AF487956

BUILDING YOUR DREAM TEAM

Building Your Dream Team
How to Attract and Retain Top Talent

David Peterson

Published by Game Changer Publishing

Paperback ISBN: 979-8-90158-403-3
Hardcover ISBN: 979-8-90158-056-1
Digital ISBN: 979-8-90158-057-8

www.GameChangerPublishing.com

*There are five people in my life who have had
a major hand in the possibility of this book.*

*Chris Darby, the best coach I ever had. He taught me to fully buy
into whatever I am doing and have a crazed level of passion. He
taught me to truly strive for perfection in all things and to never
settle for anything but the best.*

*Heather Halpin Beaty, the manager who saved my career. When I
was young, trying to learn how to run a business, she believed in
me. Without her, it is very possible that I may not have made it.
She had my back, fought for me to have this opportunity, and
helped me keep my doors open. I will forever be in her debt.*

*My parents. They have been behind me every step of the way and
have given me nothing but their full support. They have always
been there to set an example of doing things the right way, taking
care of people, believing in yourself, and always giving your best
effort. They truly set me up for success and paved the way for
everything that I have become.*

*My wife, Addison. Without her by my side, none of this would
be possible. She has been there through all of the ups and downs,
through every win and every defeat. She is always ready for our
next adventure, and she has supported me through it all. I would
not want to know what life looks like without her.*

Advance Praise

"The King of Culture has done it. Any small business owner wanting to build their team and reach new heights needs to stop what they're doing and read David Peterson's new book, 'Build Your Dream Team.'"

– Alex Shattuck, Entrepreneur

"David's approach to team building and management is truly on another level. What sets him apart is not only his ability to execute at a high level but also his gift for teaching others in a way that is clear, effective, and easy to replicate. I've personally witnessed David recruit, train, and develop some of the top professionals in the industry. Even more impressive, he has mastered the art of teaching others how to duplicate his strategies so they, too, can experience lasting success in building high-performing teams.

I strongly encourage you to pick up a copy of David's book to gain insight into his proven systems and processes. He doesn't just teach the principles of leadership and team development. He lives them. The results are evident in the world-class team he has built, making him a true example of success in the insurance business."

– Hayk Tadevosyan, Entrepreneur

"When it comes to building powerhouse teams that love what they do and consistently perform at the highest levels, David Peterson is one of the best in the business. As both a peer and someone who has worked alongside him in the insurance industry, I've seen firsthand his deep commitment, not only to performance but to people. He doesn't just talk about culture and leadership; he lives it. In his book, 'Build Your Dream Team,' David lays out the exact systems and mindset that have led to his repeated success across markets. If you're serious about building a winning team that's both driven and aligned, this book is a must-read. Be ready to take notes. It's packed with gold."

– Scott Grates, USA Today Bestselling Author,
Referrals Done Right, **Entrepreneur, Podcast host**

"Coach P's passion for helping entrepreneurs grow and scale their business is unmatched! If you're looking for a seamless route to properly scaling your business by installing recruiting and hiring processes, please take the time to dive into this book! We have a large and dynamic team and have implemented so many of David's strategies over the years… Enjoy!"

– Peyton Pettus, Entrepreneur & CEO

"David Peterson has completely redefined how insurance agencies build teams. He created roles our industry had never even dreamed of and has trained agents nationwide to run teams that are high-energy, fun, and relentlessly accountable. His impact has transformed the way I lead, and the results speak for themselves!"

– Matt Jonza, CEO

"Successful business ownership doesn't come from reinventing the wheel; it comes from learning from those who've already done it well. Any success I've achieved has come from surrounding myself with people who are better than me and who lift me up, and David Peterson is a perfect example of one of those people. He understands that systems and processes matter; he has refined those processes in his own business and is willing to share them to lift up others. David has shown what's possible as a small business owner, and his generosity in sharing his experience makes him a proven leader in the small business industry."

– Nora Vaden Holmes, CEO

Read This First

Just to say thanks for buying and reading my book, I would like to give you a free welcome call with me, no strings attached!

Scan the QR Code Here:

BUILDING YOUR DREAM TEAM

How to Attract and Retain Top Talent

DAVID PETERSON

Table of Contents

Introduction

I AM A SERIAL SMALL BUSINESS OWNER and father of four. My life is constantly hectic. I coach kids' sports teams. I run eight companies with well over 200 employees, and they each have their own obstacles and difficulties. People always need my help. That's one of the reasons why I wrote this book. People come to me all the time and ask, "How do I build a team? How do I manage people? How do I create a culture?"

I've done that through trial and error. I only got to where I am today because I constantly push forward, make changes, and adapt.

I now have successful companies because I've studied. I've educated myself. I've read books like the one you've got in your hands right now. For the past fifteen years, I've been a constant student, reading nothing but nonfiction books, listening to podcasts and to business owners, and attending conferences and meetings, always learning how to be better and improve my business.

I've grown a business from one employee to more than fifty with nothing but hard work and not a single dollar of business debt. I've now climbed to the top of my industry, and I retain my people. Through trial and error, our recruiting process has brought us results we didn't even know were possible. Over the last ten years, using the process I'm going to teach you in this book, we have had a 100 percent close rate for everyone we've offered a job to.

I have seen how these processes can completely transform a business, and I believe in them so strongly that I want to share them with the world and let you know you can take control of your business, too. You can build the team of your dreams. You can create a culture people never want to leave, and you can do it by following these steps.

My hope is that once you finish this book, you will know exactly what to do to transform your business into a destination employer, one others call on for advice. Throughout the book, we're going to walk through the steps and the details of how to do this, but to start, we're going to tackle mindset and what you need to believe to be successful in this space.

CHAPTER 1

Be a Destination Employer

IN MY EARLY YEARS IN BUSINESS, I operated an insurance agency and followed the path of pretty much everyone else in my field, asking for advice and doing what they did. I soon learned that none of us had really been taught how to be business owners. We had been taught our field, which was insurance, but the business part was never really covered.

We were all trying to figure out how to recruit and attract people on our own. We stumbled, we learned from it, and hopefully, we would get a little bit better, but most of us did not have processes in place. Agencies were just fumbling around, trying to attract talent. Then things would get even worse on the retention side, because they would acquire talent but not really know what to do with it. Fortunately for me, I had a wake-up call.

The corporate version of our business came to our town, and they were offering jobs en masse because they needed to fill a large building with thousands of new hires. Prospective hires did not understand the difference between the corporate side and the small business owner on the street, and we started losing a lot of our talent to the corporation. They were bigger and stronger, with better branding and deeper pockets, and people didn't really see the difference between us, so they would accept the better offer.

To make matters worse, small business owners like my peers and I didn't really have much of a process. We would put up postings and meet with people, and if we liked them, we'd more often than not offer them a job. Unbeknownst to us at the time, it was very easy to get the job because there were not a lot of hurdles in place. At the same time, we weren't treating our business as if it were legitimate, although, of course, it was.

A lot of things started happening around this time that forced me to wake up. Number one, I started having to compete against a big company for the first time. Prospects were deciding between the corporate and small business sides of the same business. I quickly realized how much stronger the big companies were because of everything they included in their offer: benefits, higher pay, and everything else that comes with a nice corporate job. We needed to act differently if we were going to compete with the big boys. So, that was the first thing that I decided to change.

Number two, my brother, who worked for me, was interviewing for a job with another large company, and his interview process took months. There were multiple steps to his interview process. Every time he made it to the next round, the funnel got smaller and smaller. He was beating out others, advancing to the next level, and they were vocal about it, meaning the company would let candidates know how they were moving along. He was even flown up to headquarters for the final interview.

Meanwhile, I had no process at all beyond sitting with local people and saying, "Hey, you know what? I like this guy. I clicked with him, so I'll offer him a job." Due to a lack of competition, the applicant showed little motivation to advance.

I saw that, with my brother, the further along he got in the hiring process, the more he wanted the job. When he got to the end, it didn't really matter what they were going to offer him. He wanted the job because it was now a competitive situation, and his ego was involved in the hiring process. This was nowhere to be seen with candidates in my hiring process.

Number three, and lastly, I purchased a personality profile to find my candidates, so I could put one more check in place. Along with that personality profile, I received a book called *Can They Sell?* When I read it, I realized for the first time that we had never been taught how to interview. We'd never been taught what a real interview process looked like. We'd never been taught how to talk to people.

So, I changed my delivery. I changed my approach. For the first time, I created a process that changed everything. That's one of the things we're going to cover in this book: the process I discovered and the tweaks I made that took my success rate from minimal to 100 percent. We've been running this process for over ten years now. In that time, we have hired 100 percent of the people we have offered jobs to.

Together, we are going to review everything I changed to make sure that when you bring in new talent, you bring in better talent. After that, I will show you how to retain that talent.

That's the goal, right? Find them and keep them. That was the other problem we were encountering: we were hiring too many people who would take the job and then leave. Easy come, easy go. I eventually realized they were not truly invested in the job because there was no formal process to support it, and hires had no hurdles to jump through.

When a job is easy to get, you don't admire it nearly as much. You don't value the position because it isn't a very valuable job in the first place. The role feels too easy to land, and it feels just as easy to leave. However, our retention rate has gone through the roof since we implemented steps candidates need to complete to ensure they believe the job is important.

You have to be intentional in how you present yourself. What are you putting out to the public about your business? What does the world see? How are they going to value you? Are they going to put you up against real companies? To do that, you must treat your company like it's a real business. You've got to get away from the mindset that you're a small business, that you can't compete, or that you have to settle for subpar talent.

You can be a destination employer. You can be like the Googles, the Facebooks, and all the other cool companies out there that people want to work for. You can compete with them by creating your own culture. You can create your own world. You just have to be intentional about it and act as if you deserve it.

One thing you need to determine before you get started is what you offer. Is it flexibility? Or making it easy for people to work with you? For us, we like to work with people on their schedules and at their locations, and we prioritize the type of job they're going to come in and do.

The schedule, the location, the flexibility, the benefits—all of these things are attractive. If you can find a way to offer flexibility through remote work, you are able to expand your business to other parts of the country. Then you're not limited to your zip code or the surrounding area, and you can recruit top talent from all over the country. Recruiting from a larger pool can yield amazing results when it comes to finding talented people.

Your goal, as a business owner, is to recruit top talent. You should always be looking for great people, no matter the circumstance. If you can fill your team with great individuals, your business will take off in ways you never imagined. But first, you must be open to recruiting in new ways. When you can recruit more widely and deeply, it opens up your business to new opportunities you may not have had before.

Here's a story about a good friend of mine who referred someone to me about four years ago. He called me up and said, "Hey, I've got someone looking for part-time work, and I'm just not open to that. I really like her, but I'm going to pass. Do you want to talk to her?"

"Yes, of course," I replied, though I was a bit skeptical as to why he was passing on someone he liked. So I asked him what the real reason was. I was trying to assess if he was attempting to palm off a dud on me. I truly couldn't understand why someone would pass on good talent.

He told me he was only looking for full-time employees and wasn't interested in anything else. Part-timers didn't make any sense to him when he had a full-time need. He lacked the vision to recruit great talent, instead solely focusing on filling his open positions.

I ended up interviewing the woman and thought she was fantastic. She had a unique situation at home with her kids and didn't have the availability to put in 40 hours. However, she was exactly what I was looking for in terms of talent and personality, so I brought her onto our team.

My thought process was that I would absolutely take a rock star on a limited schedule rather than passing one up altogether. Why would I not take someone great in the capacity that they're willing to give?

That's something I want you to think about as we close out this chapter. Ask yourself, *Am I too closed off?* Am I missing out on opportunities because I have tunnel vision and am looking for something too specific? You might be looking for a diamond while you're sitting on that pile of gold you're blind to. So, think about those opportunities you're missing. Figure out how to be more flexible. My friend's lack of flexibility and vision cost him a great employee.

You can work to attract different types of people and cast a wider net. In the next chapter, we're going to go deeper into these processes and what you can do, offer, and say to make yourself more alluring to people.

CHAPTER 2

Following a Daily Process

IF YOU WANT TO BE SUCCESSFUL in building a small business, one of the first principles that you have to understand is that your biggest resource is people. Your business will live or die based on the people on your team. Like anything else in life, you need a process to consistently grow that team and find the best people.

In this book, I'm going to detail my process for you, but I challenge you to develop your own. Write down your steps, tailor them to fit your business, and then figure out how to automate that process.

The first step is to assess your current process, or lack thereof. Ask yourself, *What does my process look like right now? How often do I recruit? When am I open for business? When am I closed? Do people understand that positions are available?* Answering these will give you a handle on what needs to change and how much.

Next, you must be open to hiring new people at all times. Adopt a mindset of constant recruiting. You don't ever want to seem closed off to hiring talent. If someone is out there looking for their next career, you want to be on their radar. To do that, you must constantly be recruiting.

So, how exactly do you do that? By making recruiting a daily process in your business. You must have a talent funnel. Whether you purchase an external CRM system or build one internally, you must have some form of management system. You must have a lead flow system.

If you just open up recruiting with no structure, things will quickly become chaotic. Recruits come in through email, phone calls, in person, referrals, etc. It will become impossible to keep up with them, and you'll start to drop the ball on follow-up. So, when I mention a CRM or a funnel, I mean you just need some kind of system to keep track of and organize your recruits. Such a system helps you see when recruits arrive and track them as they move through your process.

Your process might have ten steps. Which step are the recruits at, still at the starting line, or are they on step nine? You must have an organizational structure to be efficient at this, and that's where the CRM or funnel tool can come in handy.

I recommend you work on this funnel daily. For example, you might create a recurring calendar reminder to check your recruiting funnel every morning at 10:00 a.m., five days a week. You're going to see which applicants are new to the funnel. You'll see which applicants have moved from step 1 to step 2.

You're going to send out invites and assessments, and you'll kick out people who have been inactive for 2 weeks. For any process, you have to set boundaries. You cannot keep adding to the funnel without kicking people out, or things will quickly spiral out of control. Some people have to be weeded out.

My recommendation for cleaning your funnel is to set a deadline of ten to fourteen days. If you have not seen any movement from a candidate in that time, cut them. Go into your funnel and remove that person so that you can move on to better, more interested recruits. You always need to clean up and make room for fresh candidates. No matter how you set your guidelines, the most important thing is that you do this every day.

Never take a day off and always work your leads. Recruiting is just like sales. If people are interested in buying from our business, we should be following up with them. We should not let them wait two months before we check in. We should check in with them regularly. If prospective buyers are waiting too long, they will go buy somewhere else.

Recruiting works the same way. If people are interested in working for your company, don't leave them hanging. You must follow up with them and show them that you are interested, too.

Once you have a process down, you're comfortable with it, and know what you're going to do, the next question is who's going to handle it? I have found that small business owners are among the busiest people on the planet because they wear many hats and do many different jobs. We must be better at delegating.

It's extremely difficult to stay consistent and steady in a process if you have to do a thousand other things. Priorities clash, and things get pushed back or fall off your plate completely. Recruiting has to take priority. You know that people are your biggest asset, so you must put in the work to give them your best effort.

To help with competing priorities, I recommend either finding someone within your organization or outsourcing to stay on top of this task for you every day. That way, it can be done consistently. Make this one of the key priorities they do.

I understand that hiring someone to handle recruiting may seem far-fetched to some small business owners, but I can assure you it is important enough to strongly consider. Moving someone through a funnel is not a high-level activity. It is a task-based job that can be taught to almost anyone. Taking it off the business owner's plate frees them to focus on higher-level activities.

If you did not have to be involved in the day-to-day process of recruiting, how many more sales could you make? How many more processes could you create to make your business even more efficient? How much more training could you provide for your team? The opportunities would be truly endless.

I encourage you to find someone on the entry-level side of pay who is looking for possible part-time work (depending on the size of your company) and consider delegating this job to them. By freeing up your time and putting recruiting on autopilot, you can take your business to new heights. The recruiting specialist should not have a bunch of other responsibilities like you do as the business owner, and they should take control of that task.

Also, make sure that you're picking the right person. What is their skill set? Are they organized? Are they detail-oriented? Can they stay on top of the recruiting funnel? Are they a good judge of character? If it's someone who's going to be a part of the interview process, are they a good fit? Do they know what kind of recruiters you're looking for? This is a task you cannot pass off to them without making sure you are handing it to the right individual. You have to teach them and work with them before you can let it go.

Lastly, when is it going to happen? What time of day? What is your cadence going to be? How many touchpoints are there? What is the routine? Once you figure these out, put them on paper, and then when you put someone in charge, you can put it on autopilot. After consistently running this process for some time, momentum builds, your funnel grows, and you have more people to choose from.

That gets us to the next step, which is all about being selective. This is a big part of the puzzle, since too many small business owners are desperate for talent and accept people who have no business being on their team. Desperation leads them to make foolish decisions in their hiring process, resulting in the hiring of bad talent. If that describes you and your situation, fear not; we are going to fix it for you now.

In this next chapter, I'm going to teach you how to find the best of the best and how to be selective with your talent by playing hard to get.

CHAPTER 3

Playing Hard to Get

THIS BRINGS US TO ONE of my favorite concepts I discovered in my early years: jobs that are easy to get are also easy to lose. By playing hard to get, however, we will attract more talent, better talent, and retain it.

Realizing this concept wasn't necessarily a lightbulb moment; it happened after an accumulation of many events in my early years: improving through trial and error, seeing what was happening with the results of my business, reading and studying, reaching out to friends and other companies, and, as I mentioned earlier, watching my brother undergo his interview process at another company.

One of the first things I noticed is that far too often, especially with small business owners, the person running the interview is typically your type-A personality: someone who is good at talking, someone who enjoys being around people, someone who's maybe a bit of a salesperson. They enjoy hearing themselves talk.

Such an interviewer will do most of the talking, not necessarily intentionally, but they are subconsciously saying, "Hey, I want you to work for me." Because they want this recruit, far too often, the interviewer or small business owner will tell the recruit why their company is a good place to work, why it would be fun, and why the candidate would be a good fit.

They brag about themselves and the business, putting on a show to impress the recruit. This is a mistake, and a very common one, because this is not the point of the interview. The interview is for the candidates to show the interviewer why they may be a good fit for your company. They should be the ones proving themselves, not the other way around.

As a result, I realized I needed to change my interview style. I'm a pretty fun guy. I make people smile. People are comfortable being around me. I was being myself in the interview, but it was to my detriment. I was being too friendly. I was making it too easy for the applicant. I had to change.

So I became a bit cold and slightly unfriendly in the interview process. I wanted to make sure that the candidate proved their worth; they were the one in the hot seat. I was going to make them sweat a little bit. They were trying to get a job at my company. I didn't need them coming in and making a friend.

With these changes, the interview became a bit uncomfortable for me for the first time. I had intentionally changed my personality for these interviews, and I had to get used to it. However, I quickly noticed a change, and the difference in results was absolutely astounding.

It's still funny to me to this day, because after doing this for ten years now, I often call and congratulate a recruit and tell them they got the job, and they're stunned because they think I've called the wrong person. When they leave my office, they think they absolutely bombed the interview and that it went horribly. So I reassure them on the phone, and they are giddy that I've chosen them for my team. It's rare for them to run into that these days because far too many people are trying to sell instead of interview. They're trying to make a friend, to show off a little bit, and the process is too easy.

So, as you continue to play hard to get, make it difficult for these people in the interview. They're going to respect you more. They're going to desire the job more, and they're going to see that it's a hard job to get, which automatically makes it more important. They need to be selling themselves to you; you don't need to be selling to them.

The other thing I want you to do is think about where you can put hurdles in place that require the candidate to prove their worth. How many times do they have to overcome an obstacle in the job search? What we're doing here is setting up stumbling blocks. We want people to trip.

The reason for this is that many people, when they trip, don't get back up. They stay on the ground, and we don't want those people in our business. We want to find the best of the best. Our goal is to filter out the mentally weak candidates.

We want those who suffer a setback to get right back up and keep on going. That's who we're looking for to join our team. We're going to be intentional about making it difficult by putting hurdles in place. This way, we're kicking people out of the funnel as we go, and we're narrowing it to the top candidates. By making it more difficult, we end up talking to the best of the best when we get to the end of the funnel, the ones who have made it.

Now, at this point, you might be thinking, *Fantastic. The best candidates are meeting with me for an interview, and I don't want to lose them.* But another very common mistake occurs here: feeling compelled to make an offer to everyone at the end of the interview. I see this so often, and I completely understand the emotions involved. You found someone you love and don't want to let them out of your sight, so you offer them a job.

Once again, you just made the job too easy to get. The candidate sits down for one interview and gets an offer presented to them… too easy. I have heard from many candidates over the years that they got really nervous when I didn't offer them the job at the end of the initial interview, even though they were expecting it. This caused them concern, but it also increased their desire for the job. They started thinking they weren't good enough, so then they wanted what they couldn't have. They felt rejected, and their egos were bruised.

When this happens to us, we automatically want what we're striving for even more. This is what happens when you don't offer the job on the spot. And with this, the quality continues to improve as you get better and better candidates in front of you, and you're now able to choose from the best.

In the first chapter, I mentioned my brother. He was interviewing with a very good company for a fantastic job, but the process was extremely competitive and had many hurdles. He had to qualify in every round of interviews, and at each level, he was told what the candidate pool looked like: "It started at fifty." "Now we're down to twenty." "Now we're down to five." "Alright, you made it to the final three." Every time this happened, he got an ego boost. He felt more accomplished and important.

As he moved forward, his desire for the job continued to increase with every step.

When you do the same, by the end of the road, when they finally get to that offer, they're craving it. They know it's something they qualified for. They know they beat out other candidates and that the job is important.

No matter your field or industry, whatever it is, you can create this type of competitive environment for any position you're posting by playing hard to get.

CHAPTER 4

Being Proactive with Recruiting and Not Reacting to Need

ONE OF THE BIGGEST ISSUES many small business owners face is that they do not begin recruiting until they need someone. They either have an opportunity because of a new contract, they lose talent, or somebody's been removed from the team.

Somebody gets sick. Somebody has a baby. There are hundreds, if not thousands, of examples that could be given here, but all of a sudden, we find ourselves short-staffed. We're not able to handle the service load, we are lacking in sales, and tasks are piling up. We miss out on a sales opportunity. We may lose a contract because we're behind. We're trying to be as efficient as possible and keep as much net profit as we can, instead of going out and finding the next talented individual.

When we put ourselves in this situation, we do things we would not typically do. We act out of desperation and start allowing people on our team that we would usually not pick. We settle for what's available instead of proactively finding what we want.

Not only is this costly in the short term, but it's extremely costly in the long term because, more often than not, when we settle for below-average talent, we eventually lose them, whether voluntarily or involuntarily, and then we have to start the process over again.

How many months or years of efficiency, profit, and opportunities have companies lost because they had the wrong person in the seat? Even worse than the time and money wasted on the wrong person is that below-average people who don't belong in our culture or organization can run off good talent.

Has this happened in your company? Have you seen it happen in peer groups where you're putting up with less because you're desperate, and you've got people who don't appreciate that or get turned off, and they end up leaving? This can create a snowball effect, and unfortunately, I've seen entire businesses crumble because of it.

We have to protect our culture over everything else, and it's very, very difficult to protect that culture when we're desperate for a warm body. This is why you always have to be proactive in recruiting, not reactive.

You have to stay ahead of the problem or the opportunity so that you think more clearly and create fewer problems on the back end. You want to be in the driver's seat. You want to recruit from a position of power. That prevents you from doing anything out of desperation.

What's amazing here is that at some point, hopefully, as you go down this path, you will realize that you can create any position that you want to create. You're completely in charge. Do you want to delegate something, create a new role in your business, increase your sales force, or build a marketing team?

As you continue down this road, you're automatically creating new positions with each person you hire. Eventually, you reach a point where your sales team needs a service team. Your service team needs admin assistants. As the owner, you get so busy that you need a personal assistant. Then you need human resources, and so on and so on. As you do this, your small business becomes a medium business, and maybe someday a large one. But it cannot happen if we do not know how to recruit and retain talent, and we cannot do that if it's out of desperation, which is why we have to be proactive.

I got lucky in my early years. An opportunity came up when a small business owner retired, and one of his employees was available. Back then, I didn't have the vision or the capital to see things as clearly as I do now. I wanted to hire this employee, but I didn't want to take on all the risks, so I asked a friend to help. I said, "Hey, I'll take her twenty hours a week, and you take her twenty hours a week." And it was a great deal. It worked out for both of us. But what really opened my eyes was looking at the final numbers at the end of the year and seeing the impact she'd had on my business. The profit she had added was more than double what we had paid her in income.

I could see very clearly that she was also adding an entirely new line to our business. The light bulb went on, and I said, "Why don't I hire more of these individuals? Why don't I get people to specialize in other areas?" I immediately realized that I absolutely should.

That started a very long road that's still developing today: finding opportunities in areas that we are not yet professionals in. Maybe it's a weakness of ours. Maybe it's a missed opportunity. Whatever it is, we hire someone to go into that field, and they eventually grow in it. Then that field needs resources. It needs sales. It needs service. It needs assistants. It needs marketing. This allows us to expand and grow.

In the last ten years, we've gone from three employees to more than fifty by following this model, doing it organically, and most importantly, profitably. Now, as anyone in this world knows, when it comes to recruiting, there is no perfect system. But I can assure you that if you put these principles in place—playing hard to get, having a system, and being proactive—you can greatly increase your chances of success and find yourself with a much better team fairly quickly.

CHAPTER 5

Hiring for People, Not for Jobs

THIS IS A CHAPTER THAT I love. My agency completely transformed when I realized that I didn't have two departments.

That's how I saw my small business for so many years. I saw sales, and I saw service, and you fit into one of these boxes. Then, as we grew and got more selective and better at interviewing people, I realized that people are so much more complex than this. People have so many different skill sets, and we can choose to capitalize on them. My whole goal now is to create a job that you love. How cool is that? What a novel concept.

What if you had a job that was only filled with things that you loved and that you were good at? That's not how most jobs work. With most jobs, you have some stuff that you like and some stuff that you hate. Hopefully, you have some stuff that you love, but the majority of it you just sort of put up with. What if you could change that? What if it included only the stuff you loved to do? That's what I try to get at when I'm interviewing people.

Hire for *people*, not for *jobs*. This is the old Southwest mantra. We've heard it for years, right? Hire the person. But it's a little harder to live out unless you fully embrace it. My goal is to figure out what you're good at during the interview and onboarding. What do you love doing? What do you not like doing? I don't need to build up your weaknesses. I want to focus on your strengths.

Now, with that, I do have some principles that I'm going to stick to, as I believe every one of us needs principles. We have to figure out what we want out of our team. If we have a vision and a mission, what are our guiding principles? I have five items. They're non-negotiable for me.

Number one is a positive personality. You've got to be someone I enjoy being around, and you also need to be someone who's going to make my customers feel good. If you're going to be the face of the company, I want you to put a smile on my customers' faces. So, number one is that you've got to be a positive person.

Number two, you must have a strong work ethic. If I'm going to have a high motor and put in a lot of work, I'm going to want my people to put in a lot of work, too. Strong individuals, winners, don't like lazy people, so let's make sure that we're not putting lazy individuals on our team. If we do, they're going to create animosity in the good ones. They're going to butt heads. They're not going to like each other. It's not going to create a good work environment. So, when I'm recruiting, I've got to find someone with a strong work ethic.

Number three on my list of must-haves is being coachable. We don't want a big ego coming in and saying, "I'm too good for this. I've got my ways, and I don't need help from anybody." We've seen those stars on sports teams who think they are too good to buy into the team culture. How does that usually end up? Not well, right? So, find people on your team who are coachable, who buy in and commit, and who want to be a part of what you're building.

Number four is that they must be trustworthy. As you grow and take on more people, it's vital to know that you can give someone responsibilities and they will deliver. They're not going to do something that might damage the brand or hurt the customer. They're always going to keep the client's best interests at heart. That's massive when scaling a team.

Lastly, number five is that we must have people who are not dumb. This is kind of funny, but it's true. I don't need rocket scientists on my team; I truly don't. If you have a good amount of intelligence, are positive, have a strong work ethic, and are coachable, I truly believe we can teach you most things. However, there are people out there who just don't have it; not all the tools are in the toolshed.

Unfortunately, I've hired a couple of these individuals, and one in particular I loved to death. He was the epitome of the other four principles. He was so positive and hard-working. He was coachable and trustworthy. I would have trusted him with my newborn child (I did actually with a few babysitting outings). But he was not intelligent. It was heartbreaking. At the end of the day, it just didn't work out.

I tried so hard with him. I kept him employed for three years because I liked him so much. However, due to his lack of intelligence, I had to demote him and demote him and demote him. When it came down to it, he just couldn't do the job. There were too many errors, and he couldn't understand simple instructions.

So, while it's funny to look back on and talk about, it's also a good lesson to realize that what we allow at the end of the day will bleed into the business. It'll bleed into the culture. It'll show in the quality of our work, and we cannot allow that to hurt the company or our clients.

I truly believe that everyone has worth and everyone has a skill set. I know that if I build a team of good, hard-working people, we'll succeed. If you have all the principles that I just mentioned, we can make you successful. Even if you have no experience, we can build you up and make you successful, and that's what we look for.

It's truly amazing that now we will hire someone and not have a clue what they'll do. It's always comical in the interview. I get the question, "David, what does the job look like?"

Every time, I'll tell them, "I don't know yet. My goal is to find the best people out there: hard-working, trustworthy, positive individuals. When I find them, and I know that I want them on my team, we begin the process of figuring out what they are going to do."

As I said earlier, my goal is to make sure that your job is filled with nothing but things that you love, and we've got time to figure that out. You like sales but hate billing? Fantastic. Let's get billing off the table. If you hate talking to people, let's not put you in front of them. We'll just let you be the behind-the-scenes person and handle reports and details.

As we continue to grow, more opportunities arise to add more people. Our job is to find the perfect person for that role, and if we go about it this way, our opportunities are limitless. This is where scale really takes off: now there are more jobs available, and we need more people to fill them.

So, I challenge you to look at your company and your recruiting methods and figure out whether you are as efficient as possible. When you look for a very specific person to do a very specific job, are you going about it the right way? Or can you expand your candidate pool, invite more people, and find a better candidate?

Figure out what your principles are and recruit to that. What if you're just looking for great human beings who can bring value to your company, and you allow them to figure out what that value is? Such an approach changes everything. Not only will growth become easier and faster, but it will also take you to places that you never knew were possible.

Next, let's talk about what to do when you find that person.

CHAPTER 6

When You Find a Rock Star, Hire Them

IN THIS FINAL CHAPTER on having an effective recruiting mindset, I want to cover the principle of not passing up on great talent. The first thing I need you to understand about recruiting is that most people out there are average at best.

Just think about that. Think about all the people you encounter on a daily basis, whether you're at a restaurant, at the dry cleaners, or going through Starbucks. Wherever it is, think about your interactions and how many of them are truly memorable in a positive way.

Even think about your own circle. Think about your friends. Think about your family. Think about the sports teams you follow. Life is a bell curve, and the vast majority are in the middle, average at best. But if we follow these principles of continuous, proactive recruiting, we're sometimes going to come across game-changing talent.

It's only a matter of time. If we're recruiting day after day, we are going to find people who are just built differently. What you have to commit to, if you're serious about growing your company and becoming something better, is never passing up on great talent.

What does great talent do? Great talent transforms a company, especially a small business, right? Small businesses are more heavily impacted by individuals than large companies because those people can change everything. They can take you to a whole other stratosphere of success, whether it's individually or by bringing up others.

What if your team is full of average people right now? What happens when you bring in a rock star? What can the right person do in your company to improve the morale and culture of everyone else? Well, more often than not, two things happen.

Number one, the talent rises. They're motivated by the rock star. They do what they can to keep up with the rock star. They push harder. They work better.

Number two, you lose talent that was holding you back. You were letting average or below-average talent get by, but now there's a new rock star on the court, someone who's showing the team how this can be done. They're seeing what actual potential looks like, and now they're outed. Now you understand that people have been stealing from you by putting in minimal effort.

You realize that you don't have to put up with average anymore, so you work on upgrading your personnel and making space for the next rock star. Over the years, if you commit to this, you will continue to upgrade your talent because you're proactively recruiting. You're bringing on people you don't necessarily need to have, but you're bringing on people you want.

The more you do this, picking and choosing who you want on your team, the more successful your business will become. And you get to cherry-pick from the best.

Now, you may be in a position where you're thinking, *If one of these people came along, I don't know how I would obtain them. We're strapped for cash. We're strapped for space.*

Well, this is where you have to get creative. Maybe it's space you need, and you have to create some. Can you create a flexible schedule? Can you allow people to work remotely? Can you switch to a four-day workweek? Can some people work evenings and/or weekends? What can you do to open up space? Maybe there's a rotating desk now. Maybe someone's at home every other day.

Maybe you're limited on capital. Do you need to borrow money? Does it make sense to borrow it? If someone is truly a game changer, does it make sense for you to borrow money in the short term to make sure that they come in and change the business? As a small business owner, I will vote "yes" all day long because the rock stars are few and far between, and the cost of losing one is far greater than having to make short-term sacrifices to bring them on board. Make sure you're open to these people.

Make sure they know that you're recruiting. Make sure you're never closed for job postings, because if you are, this person might not ever see you. They might walk right past your business and on to the next one because they don't know that you're open or that you're hiring.

It only takes one to completely change the business, so find them. And when you get them, don't let them leave.

CHAPTER 7

Diversified Postings

NOW LET'S GET INTO THE PROCESS. I've developed it over the last ten years through trial and error, making constant changes, and I feel it is very strong and stable, giving me extremely consistent results for a decade now.

It starts with your job postings. We talked about this earlier: you want to do everything you can to hire for *people*, not for *jobs*. You want to find great individuals, good human beings who are positive, hardworking, coachable, trustworthy, and intelligent.

When we have a very specific job posting, we're kicking out most applicants. Think about how you can change that. Wherever you post jobs, however you let people know you're open to hiring, I want you to think about being more open, more flexible, and maybe a little more vague in your job postings. How can you attract different types of talent? If you're searching for great people, great individuals, the job title doesn't matter.

Now, you may be in a very specialized field where you need something specific, but I'm talking about the majority of roles out there that we can train for. We're looking for people with a variety of talents, so consider being a little more vague in the posts.

Also, consider more posts. Wherever you're putting up your job ads, can you do more? Can you list an assortment of positions? Make the ads as diverse as possible. Maybe you post a "sales and service," "assistant," "telemarketing," or "receptionist" position. The goal here is to catch the attention of different types of people.

I'll tell you right now that the ones who really stand out to me are the administrative assistant and the receptionist. Those get a lot of clicks, and it's very interesting. I have hired so many receptionists over the last ten years, but I've never employed an actual receptionist. These people are now my managers, my salespeople, and my service support. You name the role; they're filling it.

What I love about these types of entry-level posts is that when people are trying to get into a new job, one of the first things they think is that they have to start at the bottom. They think, "I have got to get my foot in the door to have a chance here." So, they pick an entry-level job that they think will be easier to get.

That's fantastic, because I just want to meet the person to discover whether they're positive, hardworking, coachable, and trustworthy, and I can find such people with any entry-level job post. By creating entry-level positions that many people never even consider, I get more applicants. This allows me to sift through them and cherry-pick the good ones.

Fish in all ponds. Do not be so specialized that you miss out on meeting the right people. You can do this by having diverse postings.

CHAPTER 8

Entry-Level Assessments

THIS IS THE CHAPTER where you're going to see a bit of the coldness that I mentioned earlier that I apply in interviews. I'm going to use some pretty harsh words in this chapter to get my point across, but I hope you can see that it's necessary.

We have to create minimums. Doing so will eliminate much of the frustration and heartache in your interview process. There have to be barriers to entry because, if we've done a good job of creating this diverse funnel and posting all over the place, we're going to get a lot of applicants, and that's the goal. We want to cast a very wide net, but after that, we've got to get tough and clean it up, or we will become overwhelmed and won't continue working our funnel properly.

So, we have to put some filters in place, and one of the things I recommend is assessments. There are quite a few assessments out there, and they are easy to find: personality, acumen, intelligence, etc. Then you must set your bar. On a scale of one to a hundred, I set my bar at seventy.

I want personality assessments to show at least a seventy for someone to move on to the next step in my interview process. Then I want intellectual assessments to be at least a seventy as well. If a candidate doesn't hit seventy, they'll be removed from the funnel.

Once again, the idea is efficiency and time. If you have 200 new applicants in your funnel, you can't work through every single one and follow up with them. You've got to set a minimum. You have to be intentional with that because your funnel will be full of winners and losers.

Let's be real for a minute. There are some bums out there. People are sitting at home in their parents' basement, sending you an application because their mom told them they'd be kicked out if they didn't get a job. Some people apply just to check a box on unemployment so they can keep getting their checks and not have to do anything. There are people sitting at work right now, sucking at their jobs, applying to your posting instead of actually working.

Don't waste time on garbage recruits. Once you acknowledge that fact and call a spade a spade, you can work much more efficiently on your recruiting process.

Assessments are there for a reason. They set a barrier to entry. I talked earlier about the cost of hiring dumb people. If someone scores a 30 on an acumen test, how do you think they're going to do when it comes to comprehending the job, learning quickly, or possibly being able to write and put things into words for a customer?

There's a reason to set barriers: to protect your time. If you're a small business owner, you've got a million things going on. You're trying to keep your head above water. You cannot wade through a bunch of garbage applications when a lot of them will not give you the time of day once you start hunting them down. Think about that.

Maybe you've been down this road before. How many times have you received applications and never heard from them again? You emailed them. You called them. Maybe you even scheduled an interview, and you got ghosted. How frustrating is that? Once again, it goes back to the fact that a lot of these people never had any intention of actually working with you in the first place.

So, why are you wasting time chasing these people? We can easily use an assessment in place of your time, and that will weed these people out of your funnel. It's that simple. This is where we start using hurdles and play hard to get. If a candidate can't get past step one of a minimum-level assessment, the job's not going to be right for them.

Don't chase them. Save the time and move on to the winners.

Now, my recommendation to help you become more efficient here is to set a time limit. They have ten days to complete the assessment. If they haven't done it by then, go ahead and move on. Kick them out of the funnel. The goal is to look for the hungry, passionate winners. I would argue that if an assessment is untouched in an inbox for multiple weeks, that's probably not our person.

Now, for those who knock it out and successfully complete it, congratulations; they're moving on to the second step: the phone interview. In the next chapter, we'll talk about how to structure calls so you can leverage another hurdle to filter out the good leads from the bad.

CHAPTER 9

Phone Interview

NOW THAT WE'RE GETTING into the meat of the process, you want to keep your goals in mind. Remember, you're trying to accomplish a few things. Number one, you're trying to get in front of the best candidates possible. Number two, you're trying to make sure that they're proving their worth to you, not you to them. And three, you're trying to stay efficient.

You want to make sure you are managing your funnel of recruits effectively and staying on top of each one. You're not letting people slip through the cracks because you can't follow up, and you're not wasting your time following up with junk leads.

What we've done that is unique is use the phone interview as a hurdle to make sure we're testing them every chance we get. The result is that we're continually getting in front of better and better people.

Now, you've probably done this before: invited someone to a phone interview by sending an email that says, "Mr. Candidate, please let me know some dates and times that you're available for a phone call." Then they email you back, giving you, more often than not, a few times that just don't work for your calendar.

Now you are going back and forth over email, and sometimes, this gets drawn out and wastes a lot of time. You've got two people who are blind to each other's calendars, creating an inefficiency. We've gotten rid of this by requesting a phone interview instead.

At this step, we email the candidate, asking them to call our office and request a specific team member who has access to our calendar.

Now, two things have happened here.

Number one, we've become more efficient. No more going back and forth trying to find a time on the calendar that works for both people.

Number two, we've created another hurdle for them, an action item that requires the recruit to complete work to move to the next step. It's no longer an easy pass. They have to take action and complete another task.

Some people won't put forth the effort. These are people that we do not want on our team. They don't fit into that great category that we're looking for. We're looking for the people who actually pick up the phone, take action, call our office, follow the instructions, and schedule an appointment.

Next, we're going to create additional hurdles in two ways.

First, we're going to give them homework. The employee scheduling the interview is going to let the candidate know we expect some basic knowledge from them: "Please explore our website and learn about our company. Also, take some time to understand what it takes to successfully perform this job."

Sometimes, when we finally have the phone interview and ask people those questions, we can tell that they're reading their answers. Maybe they're reading it straight from our website, or they've written it down. If they sound scripted, that's okay. At least they spent the time doing the research.

We're not looking for the person who stumbles, who guesses, or who throws out an answer we know is untrue because they didn't put in the time and effort to prepare for the interview. We want people who are going to take this job seriously.

Second, we're going to ask them to take action one more time and call us at the interview time. We expect them to call us, not the other way around. So, we'll say, "Mr. Candidate, your interview is on Friday at noon. Please call us at this number." If someone is not organized or responsible enough to complete that simple task, they are not somebody that we want on our team.

As we discussed, if we're working under the premise of playing hard to get and making the hiring hurdles difficult for them, we're trying to find as many opportunities as we can to do so. This includes making the candidate prove their worth. We can do even more of this through the following processes.

First, when we get on the phone with recruits to conduct the interview, we want to be very detailed in our questions and look for specific experiences. We don't want vague answers. We want to dig into their jobs.

"What did you do at that company? What did you accomplish while you were doing that job? Why did you leave?" We want to find people with strong work ethics and maturity.

It's very important to listen carefully to their answers and write them down word for word, because this is just one piece of the puzzle we'll have to come back to later. We want to know exactly how things went.

Ask them why they're interviewing with you and what they think the job entails. What do they envision the job to be, and why are they the right fit for it? Ask them about their managers. What's it like working with them? What would the manager say if you called and asked about their abilities? What are their strengths and their weaknesses? What would they like to spend more time doing? What would they like to spend less time doing?

Get them to clearly spell it out for you. Get details. Don't let them off the hook with easy answers. Most people will be vague and answer with fluff. Don't allow that. Be specific.

Now, in a phone interview, the most important things that I'm looking for are passion, energy, and excitement. I don't care who this person is or what they've been doing. I don't care what job they've applied for. I want somebody who is passionate about their work. I want someone who has risen to the top of their field.

As we said earlier, the majority of people out there are average at best. We can see that in their work.

However, if they haven't achieved anything of significance, if they haven't moved up in the company, if they haven't changed their place in life, more often than not, there's a reason for that. So, don't hold what they've been doing, what their job was, or what field they were in against them. Find out if they have passion. Find out if they're excited. Find out if they're the type of person who has the energy for your team. Ask these questions. Look at their personality and see if they're the type of person who can move your company forward.

Now, if you have delegated this task to others, you've got to coach the team handling these phone interviews to make sure they understand what to look for. And walk them through the process multiple times. Test their knowledge before you pass this off.

This is such an important piece of the puzzle because not only do they have to listen to what the candidate is saying, but also to what the candidate is not saying. A lot can be learned in silence in an interview. Are they giving specific answers? Did they actually answer your question? Or do they sound like a politician dodging a topic that they don't want to touch on? Teach this to your team and make sure they write down the answers exactly as they hear them so that you can go back and read the notes. This is a very important step.

Now, when the phone interview comes to a close, you should have an idea by now if the candidate is someone that you're serious about or not. If they are, let them know about the next steps in the interview process. If they're not, you can do one of two things: remove them from your pipeline, or, if they've made it this far, let them know they're not moving forward by sending them an email. Tell them it's been a pleasure working with them, and you appreciate their interest in your company, but you're moving forward with other candidates.

You don't need to get into specifics. I think it is absolutely fine to be vague. Thank them for their time and move on. But I do like to let people know where they stand so that they're not waiting for a response.

The last step is to prepare them for what's coming next: a personality profile, which we'll get into in Chapter 10. People are complicated. Jobs are complicated. I want to use every tool I can to make sure I know who this person is before bringing them onto my team.

If we're using a detailed personality profile that takes some time, I want to coach them on it before they fill it out. So, to close up this phone interview, I'll say, "I'm going to be sending you an email with a personality profile. Before I sit down with you in person, I'd like to figure out which side of our business you're on. Are you more of a service person, or are you more of a salesperson? I'd like to see some of your personal attributes so I have a good idea of where this interview is headed. Please take some time to fill this out, and I'll be more prepared when we meet in person."

We'll jump into that in Chapter 10, where I walk you through a personality profile.

Here is a link to my favorite personality profile:
https://app.ctssalesprofile.com/referral/SF-24754

Personality Profile

DEPENDING ON THE TYPE of industry you're in, a personality profile can vary greatly depending on what kind of person you're looking for. What skill sets are important in your field? You want to do your own research to find one that suits your needs. But as you'll see when you start going down that road, they are plentiful. There are many different types of personality profiles out there that'll help you learn more about the candidate you're speaking with, and that's the goal.

We purchased a third-party personality profile to learn more about people during our recruiting process. When I sit down with someone, I want to know as much about them as possible. It also creates another hurdle in our process, making it harder for people to go through the work to even entertain the job. We want to know that we're talking to a serious person. So, with a personality profile, we're trying to determine the characteristics and skill sets of these people, things like assertiveness, optimism, deadline motivation, independent spirit, and recognition drive, to name a few. How empathetic and detail-oriented are they? When I go into an interview knowing more about the person, I can ask more specific questions.

If I know someone lacks assertiveness from their profile, I can ask questions about it to see if that's something we can overcome and coach on or if it's something we need to move away from in the job. I might think, *Hey, this is something this person just doesn't have in their skill set*, and move on to other areas. You can see how personality profiles can be extremely helpful in allowing me to structure specific questions and learn more about an individual in a short period during the interview process.

Recruiting is one of the most difficult things in the world. You are only getting brief glimpses into the character of the person sitting across from you. You also know that they are putting their best foot forward and, many times, are not showing you the true version of themselves. They want to hide all their skeletons. They want to make themselves look perfect, and some people are better at this than others.

You don't have enough time to truly get to know them. You have to decipher what's real and what's not, and that's where a personality profile helps. The profile gives you a bit more insight into who this person actually is and how they tick. Now it's your job to find a profile framework that works for you. When you do, you will immediately see how impactful it can be.

One thing I recommend when using personality profiles is to make sure you find one that cannot be easily manipulated. Some are better than others. Some are pretty easy to see through. For example, if I'm interviewing for a sales job, I may have a decent understanding of the type of personality traits I would need to be successful in sales. I can clearly see the direction that the question is headed, and I can tell the interviewer what I think they may want to hear.

Some of these exams are hard to manipulate, though. I recommend that you play around and find one that you think fits well but is not easy to manipulate. That way, you're getting the correct read on somebody. It shows how much variance there was in their answers. What was their response distortion, and how reliable are the results? Mine will straight up tell me, "You cannot rely on these results whatsoever." Knowing that, it's really helpful for me to go into an interview. I know that, more than likely, if they have lied on answers, I can now ask some questions that test if they're going to lie some more.

This is actually one of my absolute favorite exercises. If a candidate has a very low reliability score on their personality profile, it's a red flag to me. It suggests the candidate may not have been very honest in their answers. They want to come off as the perfect candidate, so I might throw a few new questions into my interview.

One of my favorites is asking the candidate to rank their confidence on specific words: "On a scale of one to ten, how confident are you in this word?" Then I'll throw out multiple words, and I'll add a couple of fake ones: words that just do not exist. By doing this, I'm doubling down on these test results by asking: if I ask them a question face-to-face, will they still lie?

If they tell me that they're highly confident in the fake words, remember the five principles I gave you in Chapter 5. One of them is being trustworthy. If a candidate lies on their personality profile and then lies again in the interview, would you say they were trustworthy? Would you want that person on your team? That's your decision, but for me, the answer is no.

If you want to have a little fun with it, once they say that they are ten out of ten confident in a word that doesn't exist, go ahead and ask them to give you the definition or use it in a sentence. But in all seriousness, the personality profile reveals the candidate's skill set. Are they good with deadlines, assertive, optimistic, and detail-oriented? Do they have high self-promotion? Are they compassionate and caring?

There are no right or wrong answers. This is just who a person is. What it tells you is how to *work* with this person, coach them, and develop them. When are you working with their strengths, and when are you running up a hill? Certain things are going to be much harder for some people than for others. If I know you are a low-analytical person, maybe I shouldn't put you in a seat that requires high-detail orientation. It's a simple change for me as the business owner so that I can put my resources where they're needed. I want to use your strengths.

The other thing it can tell me is if someone is cut out for the job. Now, one piece of advice I'll give you on personality profiles is to remember that they're not perfect. They give you a preview of someone, a bit of a look-see into their mind, but they don't have all the answers. Keep that in mind.

If someone has taken the time and effort to go through a personality profile, complete a phone interview, and take assessments, I'm not going to kick them out for what I might interpret as a bad score. I'm going to meet with them. I'm going to spend time with them and ask them questions that corroborate the results of the personality profile. If they're a low-analytical person, let's ask some questions about that and confirm whether it's true.

However, I strongly advise not using the profile as a barrier to entry. Meet with the people, get to know them, and verify the scores. Then back the results up with thoughtful questions based on what you're looking for. I truly believe a strong personality profile can give you so much more of an edge when it comes to being an interviewer, giving you insight into things that you might not ever pick up on and allowing you to have more confidence going into an interview to make sure that you are in the driver's seat and getting the information that you truly need to judge a candidate.

Next, let's get into this interview, and I'll give you some advice on how to run it.

CHAPTER 11

In-Person Interview

THIS IS WHAT EVERYONE has been waiting for. It's also where I believe so many people drop the ball, because not many people have ever been taught how to interview someone.

As I said at the beginning of this book, interviewers often like to show off a bit during the interview. They want to make sure that a candidate thinks their company is a great place to work, that it's going to be fun, and that they should want this job. They end up selling to the candidate when it should be the candidate selling to the interviewer.

The candidate is the one in the hot seat. They're the one trying to prove their worth to the company: "I am your next candidate. You should hire me." But far too often, the interviewer is the one doing the majority of the talking, and this has got to change.

In this chapter, we're going to get into how to do that. If you do, it will change everything about your recruiting process.

So, let's get into it. The first thing I recommend is to have someone else conduct the interview with you. Now, I prefer someone of the opposite sex. This ensures that you're getting two very different viewpoints. You're going to interpret body language and answers differently. You're going to think differently about questions to ask.

Whoever conducts the interview must have another employee in the interview room with them. I would also make sure that the person is coached on what the interviewer is looking for. What kind of answers do you want or not want? What are you looking for with body language?

Give them permission to get involved: "If you see something you want to jump on, get in there. If you have a question that's bugging you, go ahead and ask it." Enable them to be an asset. Don't just have someone in the room for the sake of having someone in the room. Get them involved and make them an ally. Also, make sure they understand who is being interviewed and why.

I've got people on my team who serve a great purpose in their current roles, but they might be horrible in others. For example, I've got some young people on my sales team who live for the weekend. They make sure to crush it during the week so they can go out and party on the weekend. They're great in sales, but they might not be fit mentally or maturity-wise for an executive assistant or manager position. They might also not be the best choice for thorough, in-depth reviews with clients. Different mindsets have different mentalities. Make sure that the person being interviewed understands such differences and what you're looking for.

In the interview, your goal is to determine whether this is the best person for the job. You're not there to make a friend, get someone to laugh at your jokes, or sell yourself and your company. You're there to make sure that they can sell themselves to you. This is going to be the hard part for most people, but you've got to do the interview the correct way, and although you might be that fun, positive, upbeat person, but don't be that in the interview.

You can't make it too easy for the interviewee. You're going to have to make them work, so you need to be a little cold, slightly unfriendly. You don't want to be mean, but make the interview another hurdle.

As we talked about from the very beginning, one of the biggest principles that I want you to remember is that we're playing hard to get. Jobs that are easy to get are easy to lose. We're not going to be one of those. This is a hard job to get; there are multiple steps.

The candidate is competing against multiple people. They have to earn the job because, when they feel that way, they value it more. They're much more ready for an offer. They desire the offer, and when they get the job, they're not looking for a way out. They accomplished something, beating out the other candidates. They won't feel that it's easy to walk away.

I want you to go back in time to the last time you were in an interview. You probably got a little anxious, right? You made sure you looked good, your resume was printed out on nice paper, and you showed up early. You prepared what you would say and considered the questions you might be asked. It's not a very fun process. Not many people look forward to interviews.

So, take those feelings and make them a little more extreme; make the interview cold, uninviting, and unfriendly. However, after interviewing for over a decade, I know I'm going to make recruits even more nervous than they already are. Because of that, I do start off a little easy. I don't want them so nervous that they can't be themselves. Have you ever felt that way? You clam up and can't get the words out, jittery, not able to be yourself because of your emotions. I don't want that to happen. I still want to see the real person.

Everyone likes to talk about themselves, so I start every interview the exact same way. I greet them, sit them down, give them a timeline for the interview, and explain what the interview will look like. Then I say, "Mr. Candidate, I've got your resume here. We're going to get into it. We're going to talk about your jobs and what you've been doing. But before we do, I'd love to know a little bit more about you. Can you tell me about yourself, maybe some things I don't know from looking at your resume?" Hopefully, this allows them to open up and have a trustworthy conversation so they're not a big ball of nervous energy.

Some people will need guidance, because I am asking for personal stuff that's not on the resume. This accomplishes multiple things. It calms them down, and it gets them to open up, but it also tells me more about them as individuals and who they are outside of a job. Let's figure out who the person is.

When they do start discussing past jobs, this is where I'll guide them. If they dig into their resume, push them back onto the path you want them to go. "Hey, that's great. We're going to get into the work. But I'd love to know more about you. Talk to me about you personally. Tell me about your family and your hobbies, things that I don't already know." Most people can do this, and they will open up because they feel a little more at ease.

Then move on to more difficult questions. Be very specific: "Why did you take such-and-such job? What did you do there? What did you accomplish? How did you leave it better off than when you started it? Tell me about your manager. What was their feedback to you? If I call that manager and ask them about you, what would they say? Why did you leave?" Be very specific, and make sure that you're getting detailed answers.

I said this earlier: vague answers are not good. Typically, that means the person may be covering something up. You will have more success in the interview than you've ever had before if you don't allow vague responses. It may be awkward, but you'll get used to it. If someone gives you an answer that you don't love, ask the question again in a different way. If they still have an answer, ask it again. I promise you, it will change everything if you keep asking the question until you get the answer you're looking for.

Interviewers usually accept vague answers because they don't want things to feel awkward. Think about any political conversation you've heard, whether it's a debate or an interview with a news anchor. How many times have you seen the interviewer ask a question, get an answer that has nothing to do with the question, and then move on to the next one? And the whole time, you're screaming at your TV, "He didn't answer the question!"

Ask it again. Call the candidate out on not giving you an answer. This is your interview. Double down or triple down until the person gives you an answer. I promise you, when you get comfortable doing this, it changes everything. The skeletons start to come out of the closet. You start to see that most people hide in an interview, and you get to the bottom of who this person really is and whether they are good or bad at their work.

As we discussed in Chapter 5, one of the five principles is that we want to hire coachable people. While reading that chapter, you may have asked yourself, "How do we find that out in an interview?" Well, I'm about to tell you. One of my favorite things to do in an interview is to give the candidate what I call a cheat sheet.

Many people are not coachable because they have too big an ego. They think that they know how to do things better than everybody else. They already know this stuff, and they don't need to learn it again. It's their way or the highway. We all know these kinds of people. They're culture killers, and no one wants them on their team.

We can find that out in an interview, and there are many ways to see it. Maybe you are picking up on ego in their answers, maybe they're too vague, or maybe their answers don't line up, and they've contradicted themselves a few times. While they're spinning webs, you notice they start to trip over themselves if you're paying enough attention. So, let's attack it. Let's poke the ego and see what kind of reaction we get.

Remember, people are already nervous. They're already anxious in this interview, and they're not going to do well if you start attacking their insecurities. That's why they're giving you vague answers, and their stories do not match up. They're covering up something, and anything they're covering, they're not going to be very confident about.

So, what happens if you talk about it? This is what I do. I'll try to interrupt them. I do that intentionally because it's poking the ego. If they're in the middle of answering a question and I don't like where it's going, or I've already heard too many things that have made me pull out my cheat sheet,

I'll interrupt them and say, "Mr. Candidate, I'm curious. Do you want the cheat sheet for the interview?"

They'll look at me like I have two heads, and I'll say, "I'm serious. Do you want to know how to get the job?"

They always respond with, "Yes, sir, of course."

"Well, here's the deal. For the position, we've had over a hundred people apply." I say it intentionally, and their eyes grow wide as they realize just how competitive the process is.

Then I'll say, "Yeah, I know. It's a big number, right? So, as you can imagine, we've been very busy interviewing. Now, here's the deal. To have a shot at this job, I need to remember you among these hundred people, and for me to remember you when we're done, I'm going to have to trust you completely.

"And I'll be honest, I'm not there yet. A few of your answers haven't lined up. I've asked you a few times for examples, but your stories or answers have been vague.

"So, moving forward, if you do want this job, if you want a chance to work at our company, I'm going to need you to be brutally honest with me. When I ask you a question, I want a direct answer. I have a feeling that you're trying to come off as perfect. I don't like perfect people; they freak me out. I like honest people. For you to have a chance here, I need you to trust me so that I can trust you. Is that fair?"

Now they always say, "Yes, sir." However, they don't always back that up.

Usually, one of three things happens:

One, they adjust their responses to my request, and that's what we're looking for. We start getting direct, honest answers. That's fantastic. They took our coaching.

Two, and this is the most common reaction, they continue with their vague, fluffy, non-direct answers. This shows us that they're not coachable.

Three is possibly my favorite, because it's fun. Now, obviously, my actual favorite thing would be them following the coaching and us getting a great candidate, but number three is entertaining, at least. Number three is when you find that person who truly does have an ego problem and is not coachable at all.

When you attack the ego of someone with that personality type, they get defensive. They get angry, and you see that immediately. They start to puff their chest up a little bit, get a little color in their face, and give very short answers. You can hear an edge to their voice.

One reason I like this option is that, as soon as I see it, the interview is over. I don't have to waste any more of my time on this person. They have clearly shown that they do not have the maturity or the ego to be on this team. If they cannot handle a tough question in an interview, how do you think they're going to handle a tough job?

As soon as you see that kind of response, tell them, "Mr. Candidate, I greatly appreciate you coming in today. It's been a pleasure sitting down with you and getting to know you better. I don't have any further questions. I'll follow up with you within the next week on our decision."

You don't have to end the interview rudely and can do it very nicely and professionally. The point is that the moment you see you won't be working with the candidate, do not waste any more time on them.

Challenging the candidate in this way tests for coachability, which I think is so important because every team needs coachable people. Most people have no idea how to look for that. This is your way.

I'll share a great story with you on how this works in real life. I had a candidate years ago, a young kid just out of college. He was well dressed, wore a suit and tie, had his resume, and was having a fantastic interview. He held himself accountable for his weaknesses, didn't talk negatively about any jobs or employers, and gave me specific responses to my questions.

I started to get a little nervous. I thought, *He hasn't given me an opportunity to use my cheat sheet, but I've got to test if he's coachable or not. How am I going to do it?* Then I saw an opening, so I just threw it out to see if it would work.

While this kid was doing a great job, he was extremely nervous. I could see his hands shaking. He was jittery the entire interview. He would start to button his jacket but not actually button it. Instead, he would pull it together, fumble with the buttons, and then let it go. I knew it was a nervous twitch.

If you're nervous, what's the last thing in the world that you want? You don't want someone calling you out on how nervous you are. You're just praying that no one sees your hands shaking. So, I said to myself, "If I'm going to attack the ego, this is my chance."

I interrupted him, as I always try to do, and I said, "You're really nervous, aren't you?"

"Yes, sir," he stammered.

"Hey, it's no big deal," I said. "It's an interview. I know it's tough, but here's the deal. You're so nervous that you're jittery and shaking, and it's starting to distract me. It's actually throwing me off a bit, and I'm having trouble deciding which questions to ask you. So, to help us both out, can I ask that you not touch your jacket again for the rest of the interview?"

How's that for poking the ego a little bit? You know he was insecure about being nervous, and he'd just gotten called out on it. In his response, I saw exactly what I was looking for in this kid. "Yes, sir," he said, and for the next thirty minutes, he glued his arms to the armrests of that chair and didn't move again. I ended up hiring him, and he was one of the most coachable individuals I've ever had on my team. He could get off a call, and I could dig into him on every mistake he made, and he would say, "Yes, sir. What exactly could I have said differently to be better?" He didn't shy away from it at all. He wanted to improve, and he didn't have an ego that got in the way. He asked for help, and he got better because of it.

So, I'll challenge you. Find your cheat sheet. Figure out how to challenge these individuals and determine whether they're truly coachable.

But now it's time to drop your ego. It's time for them to ask you questions. This is where some business owners can develop an ego and think, *Who are you to ask me that question? I'm the one in charge here.* But a great candidate asks great questions because they should be selective about the job they're taking. They should be looking for the best opportunity for themselves.

Does this company offer benefits? What does the pay plan look like? What does the schedule look like? What are the opportunities for advancement? Let them ask the questions. Put your guard down, move your ego to the side, and understand that great candidates ask great questions, so let them ask. Pay attention to these questions, as they're very important. They tell you a lot about the value of the person in front of you.

Much too often, candidates get this far in the process, jump through all these hurdles, and the business owner or interviewer thinks, "They've proven themselves. I like them. Let's bring them on."

Don't do that. It's too early. You still have work to do to make sure that the candidate is the right person for you, and offering the job on the spot is one more sign that the job is not as valuable as it should be. You're going to have to make them wait a little bit longer. When you do, their desire for the job increases even more. Often, they're shocked when they don't walk away with an offer. That's good for you because it means that they want the job even more.

You're now at the stage where you ask for references. My recommendation is to ask for at least three professional references. Tell them, "You've done a fantastic job and are moving to the final round. We are strongly considering you for a spot on our team. The last step is that we speak to some people about your work history. I'd like to speak with three professional references. Please send them over to me."

One of two things is going to happen. Either you're going to get the references, or you're not. If you get them, that's fantastic. Let's work on them, which we'll cover in the next chapter. If you don't, it's sad to say that even though the candidate made it very far, they didn't make it to the finish line. If you do not receive references, no matter how much you like the person, you're removing them from your pipeline. If they cannot go through all the steps to get the job, how hard are they going to work when they have it?

Strongly consider remote employees if you are in a high-cost-of-living area.

Side note for hiring remote employees: For employers considering virtual or hybrid options, or who are interviewing people from another city or state and can't be there in person, I love the ability to do a virtual interview. I recommend keeping everything the same, and having a camera is mandatory. I will not conduct an interview unless I can *see* the candidate. I have to pick up on body language and how they physically react to my questions.

Virtual interviews can be beneficial and really helpful when evaluating someone's competencies for a position. If they're looking for a remote job, you can see on the spot how they interact with technology.

I just did an interview on Saturday. Someone wanted a remote position, and we set up a virtual call on Microsoft Teams. For the first five minutes of the call, I watched him struggle to figure out his audio settings and turn on the microphone. That tells me a lot about his ability to manage a remote position effectively.

As you can see, it can sometimes be a benefit to do the interview virtually, so I recommend not reflexively shying away from this. Be open to any type of interview as long as you can see the candidate.

CHAPTER 12

References

LET'S DISCUSS THE HOT TOPIC of references. Many people say you have to ask for them. Others say that they're absolutely pointless. Why are there two such different views on references? Well, I'm going to refer to my wife on that one.

Many years ago, we had the pleasure of working together, which was amazing. We would drive to and from work together, and with a thirty-minute commute, we had plenty of time to break down the day and discuss things.

One day, we were talking about interviewing. As I was telling her about the candidates I had spoken with, she asked me, "David, why do you even call references?"

"What do you mean?" I said.

"Well, they're not real," she replied. "I mean, if I were interviewing with you, I could easily give you Sally Doe as a reference, and in reality, it'd be my mom. I could talk to my mom, and we could create a story about the last job I worked and say she was my manager. We'd practice it, and she'd come up with all these great answers, and you would never know that it was my mother. It'd be some made-up person at a job, and she would do nothing but say amazing things about me."

"You know what?" I said. "You're right. But I would get through that person because I understand that I'm being set up."

That's how I want you to go into every single reference check.

I want you to believe that you are being set up, that the person on the other end of that phone was strategically placed by the candidate to ensure that good things were said about them.

I mean, think about it. Who wouldn't do that? What candidate wouldn't put someone who thinks about them in a favorable way in the reference position? So, you have to know going in that you're running uphill. You've got someone who likes the person you just interviewed and will talk favorably about them.

But this is the other thing that I want you to realize when you're going into that interview: You're also talking to a human being, and I have found that most human beings are good people.

So, what does that mean? Well, it means that even though the reference wants to protect their person and take care of them, they also don't want to outright lie. They are probably in a position where they've had to do this. If they were listed as a reference, there's a very good chance they were a manager or a small-business owner, and they know how difficult it is to recruit and manage people. So, they sympathize with you.

So, you've got two things in your favor: they sympathize with you, and they don't want to outright lie. However, they're going to do everything in their power to protect their person. Knowing these things, we can overcome these challenges by being extremely detailed and intentional with our questions. If I know that the person I'm talking to is going to try to mislead me, it's going to change how I ask questions. Just like in the interview, I'm not going to allow vague answers. I'm going to be specific.

The real magic is when you listen to the things you're not being told. If they don't answer your questions, it's a red flag. If they don't return your calls, it's a red flag. If they don't respond to email, they're telling you everything you need to know.

Here's an example of this. I told you earlier in the book not to hire dumb people. It's sometimes very hard to determine that in an interview. Back before I had a process, I hired a dumb person. To this day, I still remember the reference check. The candidate had worked as a bank teller, and I spoke with the bank's manager.

Here's the deal. The person I hired had every *other* thing you look for in a candidate. He was hardworking, trustworthy, and coachable. He was positive. I mean, he was an absolute delight of a person. He was awesome. Unfortunately, he was not very intelligent.

I called that reference and asked questions about this person, and the reference didn't say a single negative thing about my candidate. Now, I told you this was back before I had processes, so I wasn't listening to what he wasn't telling me.

In hindsight, I can see it as clear as day. No matter what I asked about, whether it be the candidate's work ethic, abilities, or success, the reference gave me two answers: the candidate took pride in his appearance, and he was punctual.

He gave me those two answers in many different ways because I asked him many different questions. He would tell me that the candidate was never late, always reliable, and at his desk on time. He was well-dressed. He looked good. He was professional. But the reference never directly answered the questions.

I loved that kid. I worked with him for too long because I wanted to keep him on my team, but he was never able to do the job well enough because he wasn't intelligent enough. I would have known that and would have seen through the reference check if I'd had the tools early on to understand that I was being set up and that the person that I was speaking to, while never lying to me, was protecting the candidate and stretching the truth as much as possible.

So, I challenge you. Call your references. Understand that you're going into a difficult conversation because you have to read between the lines. You have to be intentional and detailed with your questions.

Ask them to rate the person on a scale of one to ten. Ask them what the candidate's responsibilities were. Ask them how their performance was measured. Ask them about their strengths and weaknesses. Describe the job that you're considering and ask them how the candidate would do there. Ask them how they would recommend managing this person. Ask them if they would rehire the candidate. Be detailed. Get direct answers and listen to what you're not being told.

Another note on references: Make sure you request professional references. You want to speak to someone with whom they have a professional working relationship, preferably a manager, supervisor, or business owner. You want to speak to people who understand our position and can speak to their work performance. And I'll let the candidate know: while I'm sure their parents absolutely love them, they're not who I'm looking to talk to. I would like to speak to past managers, supervisors, or business owners. And if they can get us three, they should.

Now, I do understand that there are rare occasions in entry-level positions when people may not have that. Let them make that decision. See how creative they are. I've had people give me teachers, coaches, and family members when it's absolutely necessary.

See what they come up with and don't necessarily help them too much. As long as you have told them what you're looking for, give them the chance to show you what they can come up with.

CHAPTER 13

What to Do When You're Not Sure

SO, YOU'VE GONE THROUGH all these steps, and the candidate has successfully cleared your hurdles, but you're still not sure if they're the right person for your team. This happens periodically, and when it does, I have found that three different systems work well for us.

Number one is a panel interview. They have completed a successful interview with you. You have done the reference check. You like them, but there is still some lingering doubt. You are just not 100 percent sold.

Bring them back in to meet your team. How are they going to work with your people? Are they going to fit into your culture? What's amazing here, and I've done this many times, is that you can get a completely different candidate on the second go-round. I have seen people I thought were great fits come back, do a panel interview, and totally bomb. Then my team would look at me like, "Why did you bring this person in and waste our time?"

It is amazing how drastically some people can change. Maybe they are mentally and emotionally prepared for one person, but when you put them in front of four, five, or six people, they don't know where the

73

questions are coming from. They're on guard, they're defensive, and they're not as strong as they were in that first round.

For whatever reason, that panel interview can throw people off and help you see their true selves a little more clearly. So, if you can, bring in multiple people and sit down for an interview. It might even be off-site. Maybe you take them out for coffee or take them to breakfast or lunch with your team and let them ask the questions and see how they interact. This can be very eye-opening and work out really well sometimes.

The second system, one I really enjoy doing, is a working interview. Pay them for an hour of work. Depending on the laws in your state, make sure you know whether you must pay them; that will vary by location. But bring them in for an hour-long working interview and see what they're made of.

This is how I like to handle it: I give them a little bit of training. Not too much, not too little, but just enough for them to figure it out. They still are going to have some small questions, but that's the point. I want to see if they can adapt and overcome. Can they figure it out and get the job done? Or do they just stall out? Are they making errors? Are they tripping over themselves? Can they not get the words out? Are they too scared to move forward? That's the one that you see more than anything else: they're too scared to move forward. They just freeze. And that'll show you pretty quickly if it's the right person.

Option number three: Give them a short-term contract. It's a working interview, but more than the hour-long one. Hire them for ten days or thirty days. It's a temporary contract and nothing else. This way, you can give them a little more training, put them to work, and see over an extended period if they can be successful or not.

This has saved us a lot of heartache. It's still a financial commitment and a time commitment. I understand that. When you've got someone who has potential but still too many questions about them to feel comfortable bringing them on permanently, bring them on for a short-term contract.

Be very upfront with them about it. Say, "We like you. You've got a lot of potential, but there are some concerns that we have. To be a full-time member of our team, we need to see if you've got what it takes. So, you've got thirty days to prove it to us. We're going to give you everything you need to succeed, and we're going to watch how you work and see what kind of success you have. If you can do it, you'll get a permanent position with us. If not, hey, that's also great. We'll both find out that this isn't for you, and then you can move on to a job that you're much better suited for and where you'll be a lot happier."

This can pay massive dividends. If it's the wrong person, you're off of them very quickly. You won't string things out or waste more time or the company's money. On the flip side, they might be fantastic. They answer your questions, and you no longer have concerns. Once they have proven themselves and settled your doubts, you can bring them on as a full-time, permanent employee. This is far less risky for the company, and everyone wins.

So, if you're still unsure after all these steps, remember that there are still some things you can do to calm those concerns and figure out whether they're the right person for your team. Switch it up, do something different, and see what works for you.

CHAPTER 14

Time to Sell Yourself

IT'S FINALLY HERE, the moment you've waited for, possibly for weeks. You get to be yourself and let your personality out. You get to be the happy guy or girl. You get to put a smile on your face and sell.

You get to tell the candidate why they're so great. You found your person. You've gone through all this work. Your candidate has risen to the top, and you know that you want to bring them onto your team.

Now comes the fun part: you get to let them know. You get to reach out, congratulate them, and share a little about what's going on at your company, why it's such an exciting time, and why it's a great opportunity for them to join you.

I like to make phone calls, but an email will suffice. I'll let them know that out of the x amount of candidates considered, they are the person. "Out of the hundred people we had in our pipeline, we've decided that you're the best fit for our team. We are so excited about you. We think that this position is going to be great for you, and you're going to be really successful."

You can talk about everything you have going on: "Let me tell you a little bit about us and why this has been such a highly contested position. You know, we've been in the industry for this long, and we're moving into this space. Out of all our peers, this is where we rank. This is the number of people we have. This is what we've grown to…"

You get to talk about you, your business, the opportunity for them, and the possibility: "This is the reason I want to bring you on board. This is where I think you can take us. This is the direction we're headed. This is the opportunity that you're about to walk into and take over."

Next, throw out some of the perks. What do you do as a company? Why do people come to work for you? Is there a flexible schedule? Is there something special about your paid time off? Your pay plan? How do employees move up through the company? Do you hold fun team outings? Can people qualify for trips or bonuses? What makes you special? What makes you fun? How do you stand out from the crowd?

This is your chance to sell yourself. It's time to be different, and you can show off a little bit. So, go ahead and put this all on paper and practice it. Figure out what makes you different, what makes you stand out, what allows you to compete with the big boys, and make sure that when someone asks you why they should join your team or why you're different, you know how to sell it.

CHAPTER 15

Make a Professional Offer

AFTER YOU HAVE CALLED or emailed the candidate and shared the good news that they'll be joining your team, it's time to close the deal. I recommend scheduling an appointment for them to come to your office so you can do this in person. If they're a remote candidate, set up another virtual call, but you want to be face-to-face with this person, whether physically in person or on camera.

You want to be prepared and have a professional offer. To do that, you need to have your offer typed out. This isn't a handshake agreement. It needs to be on paper, something for them to read, look at, and sign. Is there a compensation plan attached? Do they have the ability to earn commissions? Do they have the ability to earn a bonus? Are there other fringe benefits they can qualify for? All of this stuff needs to be in writing so it can be reviewed at the time of the offer.

What benefits do they qualify for? Do they get medical, dental, and vision? Retirement? Qualify for paid time off? Have the ability to work from home? All benefits and perks need to be reviewed and put in writing. What are they, when do hires qualify for them, and how do they qualify for them? These are things that make your opportunity stronger than others. You're a professional, and you're going to act like it.

Now, at the beginning of this book, when we talked about the mindset principles that you need to get on board with, one of the first things I mentioned was that you need to be proactive at recruiting. You must stay ahead of your needs so that you're not desperate so you can cherry-pick the talent. It doesn't start immediately, but once you get the ball rolling and you've done this for a while, you will be ahead of the need. You'll be adding and retaining people to the organization when you find good talent, not because you're desperate for a body.

Another perk to our interview process is that we allow the candidate to pick their first date of employment. We're not desperate for them to come work for us, and we make that very clear. Remember, we're retaining the power in this conversation. They want to come work for us. We are a destination employer.

We tell them, "You can start whenever you'd like. We have absolutely no immediate need. We are offering you this job because we want you on this team. If you want to start a month from now, fantastic. Take some time off, take a trip, and finish your job. Whatever you need to do, go do it. We want you to be 100 percent ready when it's time for you to come on board with us."

Hammer all this out in person. Review all the details, answer all the questions, and make sure they are ready to go. Have them sign off on it, and when they leave your office, scan it and email them a copy. It is now formalized, and they are ready to move on.

If you want to be a destination employer, you have to act like one. That means documenting, reviewing, signing, and presenting them to our candidates. Following these steps will continue to increase your close ratio and bring you better candidates.

CHAPTER 16

Provide a Safety Net but Challenge the Ego

THIS COULD BE THE MOST important chapter in the book.

After a decade of following this process, we have a 100 percent closing ratio on every candidate we've ever offered a job to. This is due to the principles that we follow when meeting with a person. We understand what they've been through in their job searches, and we understand the BS they've been told about how much they can earn.

My first interview out of college was with some no-name insurance company offering a sales job. They were interviewing en masse, and there were probably fifty people in the room with me. They gave us a presentation where they told us, "You can make $175,000 this year," but even at twenty-one, I could see straight through it. I knew it was crap.

That was probably what their highest earner made the prior year. What 21-year-old with absolutely no experience whatsoever, no knowledge of the industry, nothing, is going to go put up numbers like that? It's possible, absolutely, but they were selling a promise that was not realistic.

I would bet you that most of the people in the room saw straight through that, which is why it's a no-name insurance company. People don't believe the bill of goods they're selling.

That stuck with me for a long time, and I challenge you to realize that you might be setting up the same type of offer. Far too often, we use words like "if you hit your goals by achieving quota." If, if, if. People don't understand if that's possible. They have doubts, so they question you. Employers see it as, "Hey, I'm letting people know how much they can achieve, that there's no cap on their abilities," but it's interpreted in a totally different way.

So, I would urge you not to promise the world. Don't promise the moon and the stars. Be realistic. Give them real-life examples of what people in your organization are doing: "This is where the good people are. This is where the great people are. These are the people who don't make it." Give them a safety net. Make them feel safe if they don't achieve their quota. Get rid of the fear and uncertainty.

But at the same time, challenge that ego. They've made it this far for a reason. They're a winner. They beat out all the other candidates. There's a competitor in there. There's a winner in there. Now it's time to bring that person to the offer table.

I want to do two things in this interview. First, I want to make them feel comfortable so they don't feel like they're being fed any bogus achievements. And second, I want to challenge them to make sure that they understand that they can make anything possible. This is how I do that: "I'm going to be real with you here. This type of job has no limit on income. You can come in here and make as much money as you want.

We've got people who make $150,000, $200,000, and more. I want to be very clear. They're really good at their job.

"Now, we've also got average people on the team. People who are good enough to be here. They put in their work. They try. They give us effort. They haven't figured out how to be great yet, but they're good enough. For those good-enough people, it's a $50,000- to $60,000-a-year job. You're not hitting your quota. You're not breaking any records. We're not thrilled, but you're doing well enough. You're keeping your seat warm.

"But I'm not hiring you to be good enough. I'm hiring you because I think you have the potential to be great. I think you have what it takes to challenge some of my top performers. And that's what I'm so excited about with you. I want to bring you on to make my team better.

"Now, I'm not going to promise you these big paychecks. I'm going to let you know they're possible. I'm going to give you every resource in the world to attain them. We're going to pour knowledge into you. We're going to pour education into you. We're going to practice and practice and practice and give you everything you need to be successful. But the rest is up to you. Can you do it?"

I'm going to challenge that ego one more time. If I have a winner in front of me, they're not going to back down from that. I gave them a safety net. I've told them what will happen if they're average, but I've also told them I want to hire them because I think they will be great. Then I've asked them if they have what it takes.

If a candidate doesn't answer yes to that question, you might not have done a very good job with the recruiting process. Hopefully, they're fired up and ready to run through a brick wall at this point.

You've got your winner. Now it's time to unleash them and let them do their job.

CHAPTER 17

Create a Plan

YOU'RE NOW AT the end of the interview process. You have had the candidate jump through your hurdles, and they have succeeded. You've decided they're the right person for the job and informed them of the great news. You typed up their offer and presented it to them. You showed them what average and great employees on your team look like and what success could be for them.

It's now time to agree to these items and sign off on the job offer, base salary or pay, and compensation plan. Maybe there's some negotiation involved; maybe there's not. Either way, it's time to close the deal, and with that, you want to get their buy-in.

Ask them, "What do you want out of this job? Now that you know that you've secured it, now that there are no more questions and no more anxiety, what does this look like for you? When do you want to start? What do you want your schedule to be? What do you want your job to be? What do you want to accomplish a year from now when we look back? How much money do you want to make?"

Have these questions ready, and talk it out because there are no strings attached anymore. Now they have nothing to fear. They beat out all the other candidates and made it to the top of the mountain. The job is theirs, and they earned it.

So, get them to sign off on your documentation. Pick a start date, tell them what it's going to look like, and prepare them for what's coming next. Do you need to order a background check? Do you need to order equipment? How long is it going to take to get them prepared to come into this role on day one and have success? Schedule the stuff out, have the conversation, and do the hard work now so that when you onboard your employee, you're both ready for immediate success.

Next, we will talk about onboarding. I think one of the most difficult things for most employers to handle is getting someone started, up to speed, and having success. Let's dive in.

CHAPTER 18

Pre-plan to Save Some Headaches

NOW THAT YOU'VE MADE IT through the tough part of finding your next candidate and securing the hire, what comes next? Unfortunately, this is where many people get a little too loose in their process and start making mistakes. They celebrate that they did the hard part and found someone new, and they start to slip up on the small details of actually preparing for the new hire. I want you to be very intentional with your time and make plans so that day one and beyond go much more smoothly than in the past.

Once the candidate has walked out your door, you have scanned in any paperwork and sent them an email with details, an offer letter, benefits, a start date, and so on, your work begins. What do you need to do to make sure that you're ready for this person to start?

Whether it's tomorrow, two weeks from now, or a month from now, you've got work to do. What is it? Do you need to order equipment? Do you have to prepare a workstation? Do you need to have scheduling in place? Do you need to notify other employees? Do you need to create anything? There's always work to be done. What has to be done, and who can help you accomplish it?

One thing I recommend is to have something planned for their first day. Do you have some gifts available? Company merchandise, things that'll help them with their job? Go ahead and plan those things out so that they're actually ready for the first day.

Bring other people in on your plan. Notify the team. Let them know what you did and why. Get buy-in from other people. See how they can help you accomplish getting this person on board.

Then create a checklist. Make sure that you're tracking your progress and that everything is getting done in a timely manner. You can make this as basic or as fancy as you want. I use a tool called Monday.com, which helps our team immensely in finishing the onboarding process. With it, I can delegate responsibilities to my team, and we have a working checklist of what is getting done, what has already been completed, and what is yet to come, so we know where we are in the process at all times.

Taking these steps will help you have a much more efficient and impressive day one for this new hire so that you start off on the right foot and give them a great first impression.

If you don't do this, if you look unprepared, if onboarding is sloppy, this is the first thing that this recruit will see, and they will start to have doubts: "Maybe this company isn't run in a very organized manner. Maybe these people don't quite know what they're doing. Maybe I chose the wrong job."

Always act as though they had multiple options on the table, and never put them in a place where they're going to doubt their choice. It's time for you to show off. It's time for you to make them feel confident about picking your team, so take this part seriously and be ready for day one.

CHAPTER 19

Oh, Shit. Now What?

CATCHY CHAPTER TITLE, ISN'T IT? But how many of you reading this book have been there? How many of you have looked up to see that front door open and your new hire walk in, and your first thought is, *Oh, shit.*

We've all been there. We had the best of intentions. We wanted to be ready for day one. But life got in the way. We got busy. We got sidetracked. We weren't orderly and organized, and we didn't get through our checklist. We're not totally ready for them.

So, how do we react? We greet them. We try our best to pretend that we are prepared and know what's going on. Then we say something like, "Hey, go shadow Betty," right? That's always our go-to: "Go shadow this person. They're going to have to show you the ropes."

Then we run back to our office, frantically trying to figure out what we're going to do with this person: "I've got to get some training ready. I've got to clear my calendar so I can spend time with them and teach them the job." We frantically try to save the moment, and this is such a big mistake because it's such an important occasion. This is the first thing the new employee sees of the job, and you're dropping the ball. So, don't let yourself get here.

In Chapter 18, we talked about preparing for this moment. You should be ready for them because, on their first day, you've got to deliver. You've got to bring the energy. You've got to bring the excitement.

You've got to make them feel welcome. You've got to make them feel that everyone was ready for them to get started and was looking forward to it. A new rock star has joined the team, and you're rolling out the red carpet.

Do you have their gifts available? Are you going to have a team breakfast? Did you get people together so the new hire gets to meet everybody, or are they awkwardly walking around the office and meeting people one by one?

Put on a show. Make them feel special. Play a game. Do something to break the ice and get them to start forming relationships. Do an icebreaker exercise around a box of donuts or some breakfast burritos. Make sure that they get to know everybody.

One easy way to do this is to have everyone introduce themselves. They can tell the new hire how long they've worked there and what their job is and then share something personal about their family or hobbies, something that they do outside of work. This helps the new hire find things in common with their co-workers and gives them a little more insight into their role aside from just what the job is. This exercise also lets them know that what they do in the business is extremely helpful.

If you want to have some fun, here's a game that we have played for a long time. It's always been a laugh because it gets past the awkwardness really quickly. It gets people joking and playing around, and it helps new hires understand they're in a fun work environment. The game is simple: after the new hire has met everyone, we ask them to guess their co-workers' ages. This leads to a lot of laughs and some discomfort, but they quickly get over that and realize, *Hey, it's okay. This is a place where we're going to have some fun.* That's always been a good exercise for people to quickly get comfortable in the office.

Whatever you do to break the ice on day one, don't fall into the trap of being caught unprepared. Don't fall into the trap of telling the new hire to shadow somebody so that they can learn their job. Things like that make them feel that they're not that special. Instead, make them feel that they're not being discarded. Make them feel they're not being pushed into a big machine and that they're just one more cog. They should never feel that way.

So, make sure that you're ready for day one. Make sure you have a plan in place and start with the wow.

CHAPTER 20

Crafting the Onboarding Agenda

DEPENDING ON YOUR SKILL SET, the technique in this chapter might be the most difficult for you to implement. This one requires time, detail, and thoughtful planning.

You need to take everything you're going to teach this person and what you expect them to learn, put it on paper, and schedule it. Now, you may start with a list of all the items they need to learn, but I challenge you to make it even better by allocating time to each one. Turn it into a working schedule.

The better you can get with the details and the specifics, the stronger this onboarding plan is going to be, and the more success you're going to have with your new hires. But I will tell you that something is better than nothing. Far too often, people don't have a plan. They put people here, they put people there, and they just say, "Hey, go learn this." Sometimes they follow up to make sure the person can actually do the job. Other times, they just say, "We learn on the job, so figure it out."

I cannot stress this enough: figure out what they need, figure out what can be taught, and then put it on paper. Once it's on paper, you can then schedule it.

The next step is to figure out what you can delegate. It doesn't all have to be you. You can assign ownership to each section. If you need them to learn topic A, assign that to your sales manager. Topic B goes to your service manager. Whatever it may be, somebody can own it.

Once you get everything typed out and scheduled, it can more easily be implemented and replicated in the future, and the new hire is not constantly having to rebuild. These are the questions that you need to ask: What do they need to learn? Who can teach it, and how long is it going to take? Is your onboarding a week? Is it a month? Is it four months? It's different for every job in every industry, but you're going to have to come up with reasonable expectations for each person. You'll have different roles, so over time, you're going to want to build out different onboarding plans. I recommend starting with what everyone will need and then adding to it based on the job.

Now, one big recommendation I have on this subject is to build in diversity. You don't want people to get stuck on one thing for days and be bored to death. Maybe you have computer modules. Maybe you have stuff that is already typed out or recorded and is available to watch. That's fantastic. That helps you be more efficient, and it helps you replicate the process.

However, if they're on the computer for a week, working through modules, what do you think their interpretation of the job will be? They'll be bored out of their minds. All they're doing is watching videos on a computer screen. That's not what they came here to do. They came here to be active, make a difference, work with people, work with their hands, whatever the job is. But it's not watching computer videos for eight hours a day. So, be careful with this.

Too often, managers and business owners take the easy way out and say, "Onboarding and training are a pain in the butt. Let's let these videos do it." Then the new person gets burned out. They're sitting at their desk for a week or two (and sometimes even longer, depending on the training), and they're not interacting with people. They're stuck on modules. They're falling asleep at their desk, and they're bored out of their mind.

Remember, if they were a great candidate, they were likely interviewing with other companies. Now, what happens if, one weekend, one of those other companies calls them back and says, "We loved you. You're the perfect person for the job, and we want you on our team." Meanwhile, that person is sitting at your desk, doing nothing but watching videos all day, and they are bored and miserable. Do you think it's going to cross their mind that maybe they made the wrong choice and should take the new shiny object?

Don't ever put yourself in that position. Diversify their training. You may have a week's worth of computer modules for them to get through. Fine, break it up. Give them other tasks in between. If they're on videos for two hours, take them off and put them on something else for an hour. I'm sure you'll have some shadowing. You're going to have some on-the-job training. You'll have some activities they can do.

What can new people do to bring value to your team? Break up the monotonous, boring training with other activities. Show them as much of the business as possible. Get them involved everywhere they can be and make sure that they don't get bored.

You're crafting this onboarding agenda, so schedule it, detail it, and delegate it. Do this. Make it consistent. Then you can replicate it.

Now let's get into the weeds.

CHAPTER 21

Getting Value Out of Your Rookies

NOW THAT YOU'VE CREATED an onboarding plan, scheduled out training, and delegated who's going to run it so that you have a crystal-clear picture of what's needed and what the timeline is, one of the other things that I would recommend you do is figure out what roles the new hire can be involved in from day one.

Depending on the business, this is going to vary drastically, but in most companies, there are certain activities that people can do to get on-the-job experience. The new hire can begin helping your existing employees. They can do remedial tasks. They can perform some things without a license or certification as long as they're working on getting it.

I challenge you to get creative and figure out where these people can be active in the business. Where can they find roles where they can actually do some work? Depending on the timeline of your onboarding, they may be training for quite a while, and training can sometimes get boring and monotonous. If you can find ways to get them active and working, this checks a few different boxes.

First, it keeps it fun for the new employee. It's engaging. Each day has diversity. Doing active work is more fun than sitting, listening, and training. It's invigorating and makes them feel valued.

Second, it helps offset some of your risk in terms of time and money put into this new employee. That's the big risk we all encounter when we bring new people onto the team. How much time and money are we going to spend on someone when we're not sure whether they'll work out? That's the risk. How much are we going to give, and how much are we going to get back? By putting them to work as soon as possible, we receive a return on our investment much earlier than we would otherwise. We're getting value from this employee as they're being trained.

We discussed in the prior chapter that training should be diverse. It should be different throughout the day. It should be as active and fun as possible. So, what if we could build actual work into onboarding? What if we could use their skill set immediately? What if we could teach a skill and then let them use it? Wouldn't this be much more fun, efficient, and valuable for everyone involved?

What if they could help organize something in the office, help take work off the plate of someone else on your team, make calls, set appointments, or assist the owner or the manager, whatever it might be? What can they do without a lot of training?

Sometimes, there are a lot of answers to that question, so you should create another list here. What can be done without training? What is the quickest thing you can show them and have them get to work on? Where could they bring value to your company in short order? Who else in your company needs help? What can be taken off their plate? By doing this exercise, you will quickly see the value new team members can add, whether they're trained or untrained, licensed or unlicensed.

You can work this into their onboarding program so you get value from them on day one and reduce your risk with every new hire. Before moving on to the next chapter, I challenge you to take action on this now. Either talk to your team before moving forward or schedule a time to meet with them. Go to your high-value employees, one by one, and ask them what parts of their job they do not enjoy. What is frustrating them? What is holding you back from more success?

Once you know these things, you can determine where to place your new employee. At the same time, you'll be bringing more joy, value, and efficiency to your team.

CHAPTER 22

Find Their Passion

AS WE ROUND OUT THIS SECTION of the book on onboarding, I would like to challenge you with a new mindset principle when it comes to bringing people onto your team, and that is creating a job built around their skill set. Most companies hire people and try to fit them into positions. "This is the job, and these are the tasks that you need to do on a daily basis to complete it. This is how we will judge you."

But what if you flipped that? What if you said, "My goal during onboarding is to figure out what you're good at? What are your strengths? What are your weaknesses? What do you like to do? What do you prefer to stay away from? What if, during onboarding, I found your passion? What lights you up? What gets you excited? Then, as we come out of onboarding, we have a better idea of where you can best be used to be the best version of yourself."

Imagine this for a moment. You go to work every day, and your job is nothing but things that you love to do and things that you're great at. Think about that for a second. How much happier are you with your job? How much better do you perform? How much more income do you make? We can make this a reality. Every time we hire, we have the power to create a role. So, what if we find out during onboarding that somebody is really, really good at one thing that we do in our organization?

What if, instead of saying, "Hey, that's part of your job, but you also have to do all these other functions," we just said, "We're going to let you own this. We're going to remove that from some of the people who aren't great at it and don't love it, and we're going to put you in charge of it." Which do you think they would love the opportunity to run with?

Get all the hurdles out of the way and let them focus on their strengths. Let them run. And now you do onboarding differently. It's not just about getting someone trained up; it's also about figuring out what their true role will be. What if that was your job? Role creation, job development. During onboarding, you're not just training them; you're testing them, too. You're learning from them to figure out their perfect role.

By the end of onboarding, you create that role. Can you imagine the potential of every new hire if they did nothing but the things that they were born to do? Your company will transform quickly, and it will create additional jobs because production will be at a level that you've never seen before and will require more work to keep up with it.

This is how you quickly scale up: You have a bunch of people absolutely loving what they do. Over time, this becomes your new team. Think about it: you can change existing people's jobs, too. As I mentioned earlier, what if everyone in the office has a part of their job that they don't like? What if you went around and spoke to those people regularly, asking them, "What's holding you back? What part of your job do you not enjoy?" And what if it turns out that you have another employee who loves doing that?

What would the result be if you said, "I'm going to take that off your plate, and you're not going to have to do it anymore," and then gave the task to the person who likes doing it? What would the potential of your company look like if it were built this way?

I know this sounds crazy. It may even sound impossible to you, but it can be a reality. You can build it out. You can change the roles, and that should be the goal of onboarding: to figure out what this person's true potential is and, to the best of your ability, fit that potential to a job.

Start to do this in your company, and it'll take off in ways you never even dreamed.

CHAPTER 23

Know Your People

CONGRATULATIONS! You've got a team, you've got an onboarding plan, and now you have good, solid, trained people in your organization.

The next thing you have to worry about is making sure that you retain them. Any business is going to deal with turnover. The great ones limit it. We can minimize it as much as possible by creating the right environment.

You spent so much time and effort finding good people and training them. Now you have to keep them. I truly believe it all starts with caring. As the leader of the company, you have to be the chief culture officer. You've got to make sure that your people know you care—truly care.

Earlier in the book, we talked about your goal: to fill your team with good human beings. Well, in return, you also have to be a good human being. When they think of you, do they think of someone who actually cares for them, who wants them to be there, who makes them feel valued for their work and their effort? Do you give that off? Whether it's through direct contact or your leadership, what kind of image do your people have of you?

The more levels there are between you and other people in your organization, the more you have to make sure your culture is still coming through, that your leaders aren't changing it into something you don't want.

Take some time. Set this book down and ask yourself, *Do my people know that I care for them?* Figure out what the real answer is. From there, you've got to figure out how to improve the current status. Whether it's good, great, or awful, it can always get better.

So, how can you get to know your people better? You should always be asking yourself, *Do I know my people? How often do I spend quality time with them? How often do I visit with them?* Sit down with them and ask them how they're doing. Learn what they've got going on for the weekend. Have they taken any family trips? What's going on in their household? How's their job? Is there anything that they need? Is there anything that they want? Are they getting the face time with you that they crave? Do you know the details of their life, family, pets, and hobbies? What sports teams do they root for? Do you know these things? Do you understand how they're motivated? What pushes them to the next level? Is it money? Is it recognition? Is it an incentive?

I recently learned that one of the people on my team, whom I absolutely love and thought I had been doing a great job of leading, no longer felt respected. She's a people pleaser, which means she keeps everything inside. She doesn't often speak up, but when she does, it's a really big deal.

However, because she's a people-pleaser, she would hide it. When she asked for something, she did so nonchalantly, and as a result, her requests were often overlooked and pushed aside. From her perspective, though, she was waving her arm and shouting, "I need attention!" but she wasn't getting it.

We leaders thought we were giving her everything she needed, but she felt so disrespected that she no longer enjoyed her job or the culture and didn't want to be there anymore. When we found out she felt that way, we made the necessary changes to fix the situation, which were simple, but we had been blind to them because we had not been paying attention to who she was at her core. The truth is, we should have known better.

I had another employee who felt they were failing in their job and, as a result, wasn't happy in their position. In the leadership's eyes, however, they were doing a fantastic job. Because they were at a high level within the company, they weren't receiving much feedback from leadership. They weren't getting much accountability because they had already been given that trust and a long leash. Leadership just assumed, "Hey, everything's going great." But because this person had a very high need for recognition and wasn't getting it, they felt they were failing.

This is why it's so important for you to know and understand your people. Know what motivates them. Know what their triggers are. How do you help them get to the next level? This is where you can go back to the personality profiles that you did in your recruiting process. More often than not, they will tell you what these people need.

How do you hold them accountable? How do you lead them? How do you drive them? How do you communicate with them? You need to go back to these profiles and make sure that you stay fresh on who these people are and what they need.

If you lose sight of that, you can lose a valuable connection to your people. They can eventually become unhappy in their position and start to lose the love and passion they had for the job. Eventually, they will find something else to relight that fire, and they will leave you. This can almost always be prevented if you engage and stay on top of how these people click.

In the next chapter, we'll get into how to proactively stay on top of that and make sure that you keep these relationships as strong as they can be.

CHAPTER 24

Showing Love and Appreciation

IN THE PREVIOUS CHAPTER, we talked about creating a culture, making sure that you understand your people, that you care for them, that they know you care for them, and that you understand what motivates them. Now it's time to put that into action and ensure it's consistent.

This starts with recognition. Every person out there needs recognition in some form or another. The difficult part is that we all crave it in different ways.

So, what does that look like for each person on your team? How do they want to be recognized? Do they need words of affirmation? Do they want to be showered in gifts? Are they motivated by money? What is it? Every person has a different trigger. This is why managing people is not easy. Every one of your people is going to need a little something different. So, make sure you truly get to know them and figure out what those things are.

One thing you should do, and that so many people do not, is ask them. Ask them, ask them early, and ask them often, "How would you like to be recognized? In public? In private? How do you prefer to be motivated?

Do you like receiving gifts? Do you like having money available? What is it?" People change, and you should change with them.

Then, once you start to learn these things, be intentional about focusing on them on a weekly basis, maybe even daily, depending on how you can do so. How often can you show love and appreciation to your people? Now, some people are scared that if they show too much appreciation and love, people will get a big head, think they're worth more money, and demand a raise. Truly, some people are scared of that.

I think that's so foolish. When you have people who should be celebrated, you need to celebrate them. That's the only thing that you should be thinking about. So, give them love. Find ways to make them feel important. Find ways to make them feel special, and make sure it's a regular thing.

One of those things is a basic human need: physical touch. This is a touchy subject, no pun intended, for many different reasons. You can do this the wrong way, of course, but I'm talking about doing it respectfully. We want to treat people just like we would our loved ones. How many hours do you put into your job? It's very common to spend more time with your coworkers than with your family. You're there more than likely eight or nine hours a day, five days a week.

What I want to discuss here is returning common-sense principles to the workplace. If I truly love someone, if I truly care for them, does it not make sense to have some form of physical touch involved? Is it uncommon for you to hug a friend or a relative? Not at all. But in some corporate environments, that is the last thing that we should ever do.

We are taught to never touch people and told that it crosses a line. It's not acceptable to be physical in the workplace. I am here to challenge that narrative in a common-sense way. I believe we need to bring that back, get used to it, and make it commonplace.

I had a new employee on my team who had just lost her grandmother. She came into the office after being out on bereavement leave, and I could immediately tell that she was still down. I asked her, "How are you doing?"

She gave me a shrug. "I'm doing okay."

"Do you need a hug?" I asked.

"No, I don't," she replied.

"I'm going to give you one anyway," I told her. Then I walked over to her, opened my arms, and gave her a big bear hug. As soon as I did, she broke down and started sobbing. She ended up holding on for a few minutes, and I let her get it all out.

When we let go, I told her that everything was going to be okay. "You take the time you need. We're here for you."

And she said, "Thank you."

That was it. We moved on, and she went to work. I didn't think much more of it until later that night. I was at home, and I got a text message from her. It said, *I just wanted to thank you for taking the time for that hug today. I don't know why I told you that I didn't need one, but I did. And it really means a lot that you care.*

This is the type of thing that we're told not to do in the corporate world. We're told not to have that physical contact. We are told to respect personal space and boundaries. But remember, at the end of the day, we're all human beings, and physical touch is something we all need.

Study after study has proven that children who were not hugged enough have issues as adults. Do you think that this need stops when we become adults? Absolutely not. So, if we care for these people, we need to show it.

Nobody loves the corporate feel. Nobody enjoys the rules, the boundaries, or the stripping away of humanity. So, no matter how big your company is, as long as it's done in a respectable way, incorporate some physical touch. Treat people like human beings and show them love.

I once met a fellow business owner who was really struggling with culture. When we met, he told me that his office environment was toxic. Nobody really wanted to be there. They clocked in, they clocked out, and they got their work done, but there were no friends. No one hung out together after work or cared to socialize. It was not a fun place to be. He wanted to learn more about my culture. He had seen our social media and what we had put out there and said, "I want to learn how to do this."

So, I asked him to tell me more about his team, culture, and leadership. He told me he had seen pictures on my social media pages of me and my team hugging. He'd noticed that we always had our arms around each other in group pictures, and he could not understand how that was possible in the workplace.

I asked him why this was foreign to him and where the struggles had come from. He explained that before he was a small business owner, he had spent decades in the corporate world and had worked up to the executive level of a large company. In his world, especially as a leader, any physical touch was completely off-limits. They went through training on this every year and were always warned to never cross that line. So, when he opened his small business, he ran it the same way. There was a line between boss and team, and that line should never be crossed. He told me that on the best day, if something big happened, the team might get a fist bump. That was it.

This was a big hurdle for him to get over. After talking this over with him, I truly believe the lack of love and physical touch was keeping his business from thriving. It was preventing his people from feeling loved and appreciated because those things were never shown.

Think about your favorite sports team, whether it be football, baseball, basketball, or volleyball. Volleyball, specifically, is a great example. How often do they embrace on the court? How often do they hug, high-five, and slap butts? I don't recommend the butt-slapping in the workplace, but you get my point. There are limits, but think about these examples.

The bonds that you get on a sports team are ones that we would kill for in the workplace. Physical touch is clearly one of the things that takes it to that level. So, I recommend that you adopt some common-sense principles and bring this back in the right way.

Now, since we have pushed the envelope a little bit with physical touch, let's take it a step further. Let's continue down the road of crossing the line in a few other areas because, once you master some of these delicate things, your workplace can become a truly special environment that no one will ever want to leave.

What are the other things that you're not supposed to do in the workplace? Don't talk about religion. Don't talk about sex. Don't talk about politics. Right? Isn't this what we have been told our entire lives? Let me ask you again, who do you talk to about these subjects? You talk to the people who are closest to you in the world: your family and close friends.

Think about that for a second. You spend more time with the people you work with than anyone else, so why wouldn't you create an environment where you can talk about those things? Now, there's a right and wrong way to do this, but if we use common sense, there's no reason that we shouldn't be able to open up spaces in a safe way to have these conversations.

Doing this fast-forwards relationships. How many coworkers do you think of as friends but don't really know much about? You don't hang out, and you don't chat after work. The reason for this is that you don't get into the deep stuff with them. But how much deeper could that relationship strengthen if you started talking about these things?

You can't create old friends, right? These people don't know your phone number from when you were a child, or what your backyard looked like. You can't go back and recreate that. However, I feel that talking about these taboo subjects and crossing these boundaries can get us as close as possible to making old friends.

Now we're talking about things that other people don't talk about. This creates deeper bonds, and it helps us find commonalities. As a business owner, you have to be careful about this. I'm not saying it's easy, but if you can safely navigate these waters, you can create magic. You can create a culture people love and can never imagine leaving.

Now, sometimes, this can go too far. Obviously, for the past eight years in this country, we've seen a pretty wild political climate, with two sides that are very, very opposed to each other. I've got people on my team who are on both sides of that fence, but we create a very fun office environment where they can go back and forth and make comments to each other.

However, one day, someone said something that crossed the line in a big way. It wasn't just inappropriate for the workplace; it was straight-up inappropriate in any setting and something no one should ever say. So, I stepped in and created some barriers.

I said, "We're going to have some fun here. If we're going to talk about these things, we're going to do it the right way, and it has to be managed."

If you can figure out how to do it the right way, if you can allow a little bit of freedom and fun into your workplace, magic can happen that will allow you to retain employees like you've never retained them before because you've given them something that they've never had before, and they don't want to lose it.

You can be a destination employer. You can stand out from everyone else, and you can do so by embracing common sense and creating a special work environment.

CHAPTER 25

Create a Culture of Accountability

WE'VE COME TO THE END. Now it's time to make sure that we have a great team and a great culture in place and that we hold everyone accountable so that they can be the best version of themselves and truly flourish.

Winners want to be held accountable. One of the first things you need to realize is that people who shy away from accountability are not the people you want on your team. They're hiding stuff. They're shirking their responsibilities and trying to see how much they can get away with, and that's not okay.

You want people on your team who crave accountability. They want it. They want to be coached. They want to be pushed. They want to find out what their next level is. They want to be the best version of themselves. And there are so many ways to hold people accountable.

Once you figure out accountability, it becomes fun and exciting. It's fun because you will tweak it forever. Your team will always change, and, as you'll soon realize, everyone needs to be held accountable differently. People have different needs and personalities. Once you figure out these differences, you can manage accordingly and customize your delivery. Let's walk through some steps, and I'll give you a few examples of things that you can do.

Number one is performance reviews. I recommend early performance reviews on days thirty, sixty, and ninety. This provides a few touchpoints to see how the person is doing with training and on the job. You want to stay on top of them early so you can get a good understanding of how things are going. From there, you'll want to develop a cadence that works well for you. Is it weekly? Monthly? Semi-annually? Annually? What is it?

I meet with my employees once a year. This gives them face time and ensures we keep that culture of care, so they know I'm involved. I want to see them. I want to hear them. Their managers, however, meet with them biweekly. We'll get into those steps in a minute, but in performance reviews, employees need to have the opportunity to be seen and heard. This makes them feel special. It makes them feel valued.

Give them that opportunity. Applaud their successes: "That was great!" Find specific examples where they did well. Address their deficiencies: "Hey, we're missing the target here. What's leading to it? Where can we help you?" Get their feedback. Listen to them. Develop goals with them: "What do you want to do? What does this look like next year?"

Continue customizing that role as we discussed earlier. Figure out how you can minimize their weaknesses and focus on their strengths: "How can you change their job? How can you improve their current situation?" Then get feedback on your leadership team: "How is management? Where are they helping you the most? Where do they need to get better? What can we do for you?" These performance reviews are crucial for you to make sure you continue to move in the right direction and get the most out of your people.

We also need to have regular, frequent one-on-ones with your team. This is what I was referring to when I mentioned that my managers meet with their subordinates every other week. We're going to have a short-term cadence. We're going to meet regularly so we can be a resource for our people. We're going to coach them regularly. What do we need in our business? Make sure they align with the goals and have a clear understanding of what's happening.

We're going to coach specific items, addressing deficiencies and focusing on strengths, track their goals, look at their progress, see how they're doing, and help them move in the right direction. Are they on pace? Do we need to change course for their targets? Do we need to make tweaks to their goals? How are they doing? Do they understand the goals? Are they aware of their progress?

One-on-ones could be weekly, or they could be every other week. They could be monthly. I would challenge you not to go longer than monthly because they should be regular. Longer than monthly, and you're more looking at a performance review situation. You will miss things, and inefficiencies will develop. If you truly want this to work, don't go longer than thirty days without a one-on-one.

From here, you need to make sure you have a consistent tracking tool. You need to make sure that everything you want to focus on is being tracked regularly and that the results are easy to access. Do you have a worksheet that you're reviewing with your employee? What are you reviewing with them on a regular basis? Is any of it automated? Can the data collection be outsourced or delegated to someone on the team? Can the direct report be responsible for delivering data to you to save time and build in accountability?

Many people ask me, "How do you hold people accountable?" One of the simplest things you can do is make everything visible. Put everyone's numbers in front of the whole team. Make it impossible for the slackers to hide. When you make everything visible and you put it out in front of the team, you create peer-to-peer accountability.

What is interesting is that the accountability doesn't even have to come from you. People feel guilty for letting down their teammates. They don't want to let their peers down because they can't carry their own weight. The good performers are definitely not going to accept someone who does not put forth the effort. They're going to push them to do even more.

So, now you have a culture of accountability. You have it coming from all angles. This can truly transform an organization when it's not just coming from the top. To do this, you, as the business owner, have to figure out what activities to track that lead. What's important to the company? What activity can you control on a daily basis that'll get you toward your goal? What doesn't need to be tracked? Which items are you currently tracking that are not vital to your goal?

Don't do too much. You don't want to overwhelm and exhaust your employees. Keep it simple. Make sure that the goals are easy to understand and specific to each person's job. Don't put a bunch of numbers in front of them that they don't care about. Make sure that the numbers matter.

Once you figure out what you need to track, determine how often you'll track it. Is it daily, weekly, monthly, annually, or all of the above? I strongly recommend having some version of all of the above. What happens is that when we do it daily, we miss the bigger picture. Sometimes, we have to pull back, look at things from a wider lens, and say, "Wow. I wasn't catching this when I was just looking at day-to-day numbers, but now that I look at a week or a month or a quarter, there are some big variations between employee A and employee B. We've got some big inefficiencies over here that we need to fix." So, make sure to change your scope. Don't just look at things through a tiny hole. Expand that scope and periodically look at larger numbers. Doing this will help you get a good understanding of what's actually happening in your business.

Once you've figured out your cadence and identified what you're going to track and when, you need to do your best to automate your reports. Do you have technology that can do this for you? Is there a person on your team you can delegate it to? Can the reports be automated? Doing that can save you a lot of time and effort.

Make sure you have these numbers at your fingertips at all times. It's amazing to start a day knowing exactly what happened the day before. So, figure out if you can get technology to do it for you, and if not, find someone on your team or hire someone to create the reports and deliver them to the people who need them.

Another thing that helps is having a scoreboard. What kind of technology can you use that puts these numbers in front of your team? If you know what metrics to track and what the goals are, get them in front of people. Now, this can be as simple as a whiteboard on a wall or a piece of paper in a break room, but you want to make it fun. You want to make it simple.

You want to make it accessible and make sure it matters to every person on the team. They need some buy-in, so make sure they have a reason to look at it.

The number one killer of the scoreboard is when the business doesn't update it. You walk by it every day, and it hasn't changed in a week. That's not good because people stop paying attention to it. They walk past it without even thinking to look. So, if you're going to put up a scoreboard, keep it current and make sure it's always up to date with the latest stats.

Next is to know your goals. You've got to understand what's important to the business and its employees. Make sure that everyone is aligned with the company vision. And when your goals are completely clear, you need to make sure that they can be tracked easily and that you're staying up-to-date on their progress.

Goals are often long-term in nature, so let's celebrate the wins along the way. Let's break them down into smaller chunks and look at them on a regular basis. If you're only looking at them once a year, it's too late, so keep your goals in front of you and understand what you need to stay on pace.

And once again, make sure you have the right people on your team. When you start making these changes and putting these things into practice, pay attention to your people. Are they scared of these meetings? Are they constantly unavailable on the calendar? Are they moving things around? If they are, they're avoiding accountability, and that's not what you want. You want great team members who want your time, who want your advice, and who want to be held accountable.

When you find winners, give them what they want, keep them motivated, and continue every day to create a culture that will keep the best people in place. When you do, they will refer all their friends and family to come work for you as well.

Conclusion

LET'S RECAP what we've discussed while reading this book. The goal is to build the team of your dreams and have the business you have always wanted, but didn't even know was possible.

To do that, I truly believe you must shift your mindset to prepare for what's possible. First, you have to believe that you can be a destination employer, that you can put tangible things in place that will make people want to work for you. Once you can do that, once you start acting like a business, once you start putting things in place, such as benefits, pay, schedule, location, remote work, flexibility, and all these things, you start bringing in talent.

Second, adopt the mindset that recruiting is a daily process. Every day, I have to recruit, and I don't turn it off, even when I'm at capacity. You will recruit every day as long as your business is open, because you now know that personnel are your most important asset.

The moment you start recruiting, you're going to play hard to get. You're going to treat your job as important and make sure you recruit the best of the best. You're going to get the cream of the crop and believe that you deserve it. You can do that by putting hurdles in place and making sure that you don't have an easy job.

Next, be proactive in your recruiting. You're going to stay ahead of the need because you know that when you need someone, you cut corners, get desperate, and let people join your team who should never have been there in the first place. So, you're never again going to be reactive with recruiting. This is now a proactive process for you.

You're also going to hire for people, not for jobs. You're going to fill your team with good human beings. You're going to have a set of principles that each person coming into your business must have, and you're not going to back off on those. You're going to draw a line in the sand and make sure that people can live up to the expectations of your dream team.

Last, when it comes to mindset, you're not going to pass up on rock stars. You now believe and see clearly that the majority of people are average at best. When you find game-changing talent, you're going to do whatever it takes to get them onto your team. Whether it means offering a flexible schedule or creative pay, sharing employees, or finding funding, you're not going to miss out on these people anymore. You're always open for rock stars.

Now that you have finished this book, whether you've already completed it or you plan to do it when you finish this conclusion, you're going to create a process. You're going to lay out what your interview process looks like. How are you going to play hard to get? What assessments are you going to use? What's that phone interview going to look like? What is your personality profile? How is your interview structured? What are the reference checks going to look like? What do you do if you're not sure?

I've given you all the tips and the tools that you need to be successful in hiring, but now it's time for you to make the process yours. Get it on paper, make sure it's detailed, and then follow the plays.

We've taught you how to place an offer, sell yourself, make it professional, provide a safety net, challenge the ego, and create a plan so that you can then take it right into onboarding and make sure that you're prepared for day one. We've explained the importance of making sure that your job lives up to the expectations of this new rock star that you're bringing on, that you get value out of onboarding, put them to work, find their passion, and allow them to be the best version of themselves.

You're going to create an unbelievable culture. You're going to love your people. You're going to show them appreciation. You're going to create a workplace that they never want to leave. However, while you love them and show them appreciation, you're also going to hold them accountable. You're going to show them what it takes to win. You're going to give them all the tools necessary to get to that next level and unlock their potential, because now you know what it takes.

I challenge you to take action. Don't put this book down, think, *That sounds wonderful,* and then go right back to your normal day. Make a change. Start with something and share your success with me. Shoot me an email at coachp@coachpconsulting.com. Let me know what you've put into practice that has changed your company. Share your success stories with me. Fill me in on your journey. Let me know how I can help. I'd love to offer my assistance.

Finally, thank you for picking up this book. Thank you for going on this journey with me and letting me share my experience with you. I promise you that if you're consistent with these principles, if you put them into practice, and if you stick with them, you'll have more success than you ever imagined. My hope for you is that your business reaches levels you never dreamed of. I can tell you from experience that if you stay diligent and consistent, it'll happen. It's only a matter of time.

If you want to learn more or have a conversation, you can find me on Instagram at @savingwithdavid. If you want to know more about what we do and how we help small businesses, you can find our website at www.coachpconsulting.com.

Thanks again, and best of luck on your journey. Level up!

THANK YOU FOR READING MY BOOK!

ACCESS YOUR FREE WELCOME CALL

Scan the QR Code Here:

I appreciate your interest in my book and value your feedback, as it helps me improve future versions. I would appreciate it if you could leave your invaluable review on Amazon.com with your feedback. Thank you!